Schools of Thought

Schools of Thought

Mary Warnock

Faber & Faber
3 Queen Square London

First published in 1977
by Faber and Faber Limited
3 Queen Square London WC1
Printed in Great Britain by
Latimer Trend & Company Ltd Plymouth
All rights reserved

British Library Cataloguing in Publication Data
Warnock, Mary
    Schools of thought.
    1. Education—Philosophy
    I. Title
    370.1   LB17
ISBN 0-571-10963-2
ISBN 0-571-11161-0 Pbk

Contents

Introduction

It cannot any longer be seriously doubted that there is such a thing as the philosophy of education. Apart from the considerable volume of writings, as well as university and other courses which are produced under that title, there is beginning to be a recognizable subject matter which cannot be otherwise described. It may, as some would maintain, be a very low branch of philosophy, but there it is, none the less

A distinction is commonly drawn between the philosophy and the theory of education, the latter being concerned among other things with the psychology and techniques of teaching and learning and with comparative methodology. The theory is then held to be the concern of teachers (what they learn in their training), while the philosophy can go on undisturbed in the universities. A bow is made to it by student teachers, but then it is forgotten.

However, I do not want to draw any sharp distinction between educational philosophy and educational theory. It is true that psychological, methodological and technical expertise are all outside my knowledge. But there is a crucial area which must be the province of both theory and philosophy: both should concern themselves with questions about what should be taught, to whom and with what in mind. And it is part of my purpose to argue that such questions should be raised and debated by teachers, not just while they are training, but constantly throughout their careers at school and university. In school as much as outside it, thought of a serious kind about what is on offer and why, is an absolute requirement of a rational and civilized society.

9

There doubtless was a time when teachers could say, 'I am a specialist. I shall get on with teaching my subject and leave educational theory to the educationalists.' Or they could say, 'I am concerned with children, not theories. I will raise no questions about what I am to teach, but get on with it, and concentrate on the individuals to whom it is to be taught.' But neither of these attitudes is reasonable any longer, if only because theory has become so powerful and wide-ranging. The consequence is that there is almost no aspect of education, whether at school or university, which is not open to question. Nothing can be assumed to be valuable or worth doing without argument. Therefore if anyone engaged in the business of education is to feel satisfied, he must be prepared to think about what he is doing and why and for whose benefit. At the least, a refusal to tangle with the theories can lead to a failure of nerve, to a sense of insecurity in pursuing any particular educational policy; and nothing could be more harmful to education than that disease among its practitioners. But at worst such a refusal might open the way to a kind of education which was bad or inadequate, in absolute terms, because of a lack of readiness to criticize otherwise than superficially what was on offer. It is not only the educationalists, then, the curriculum designers, child-development experts and so on who need to consider the theory, or philosophical presuppositions, of what they are engaged in. Far more seriously, it is those who actually earn their living by teaching who need to consider such things, and this not just once in the course of their training, but continuously in their working lives so that they can check theory against practice, and modify what they once thought in the light of experience.

So part of my purpose is to urge teachers to interest themselves in the theory of what they are doing. But it is not only teachers who ought to be concerned with it. For I hope to show what it is impossible wholly to separate educational from moral and political arguments; and if this is the case, then others besides teachers must be expected to hold, and argue for, serious opinions. Not only must parents be prepared to argue for what they want their children to have educationally, but employers, consumers, and society as a whole must think about their demands and the theoretical justification of them, without being made to feel guilty of trespassing if they express their reasoned point of view. Teachers are, it is true, professionally concerned with the theory of education as the rest of society is not; but just as neither lawyers nor doctors can regard themselves as totally isolated from the rest of society with respect to law and medicine, though they are responsible for standards of practice within their professions, so teachers cannot suppose themselves to be solely responsible for the content or distribution of education, though they must be responsible for the practical execution of the theories.

This is my general purpose. I want to contribute, if possible, to a quite general critical awareness of the theoretical issues in education. By taking some central and related problems which are matters of discussion at the present time, I shall try to see to what extent any of them is purely educational, or how far, on the other hand, wider questions of value are incorporated in them. Now there are, no doubt, many kinds of values. But education is concerned with the right raising of children, and with the provision for them of a good future, and here if anywhere *moral* values appear to be inextricably involved. Moreover, since decisions on behalf of other people and decisions which will necessitate legislation are also involved, there is of necessity an element of *political* evaluation here as well. So as each one of us has to be his own moralist, and as we are not accustomed to have our political judgements made for us, it follows that each one must, to a certain extent, be his own philosopher of education as well. This may be tiresome for educationalists, who could with justice be said to be experts over part of the field. But one should not be deterred from thinking by the fear of unpopularity.

What are the kinds of problems, then, which I maintain we must all think about for ourselves? What is a problem in the philosophy of education? It might seem logical to start with a definition of education itself, and then treat as a problem in educational philosophy any problem which obviously arose within the bounds of the subject so defined. But this way of going about things would not in fact be very fruitful. A great deal of time has been spent and, I suspect, largely wasted, on the attempt to define education. Is it an activity? Is it a process? Is it a commodity which can be dispensed in smaller or greater quantities to clients or consumers? Is it necessarily goal-directed? All these and many more questions have been raised, and it is doubtless quite fun, and not bad exercise, to discuss them. But the truth is that the word 'education' is used in a number of different ways. For example, some people feel inclined to say, 'Education goes on for the whole of our lives. We are always learning something new.' On the other hand it is perfectly obvious, even to those who say this, that there is another sense in which education does *not* go on all our lives but stops after secondary or tertiary education, at the age of sixteen, eighteen, or, say, twenty-one. So then, in order to sort out the different senses, it becomes necessary to distinguish 'education' from 'education in the true sense' which is identical with learning and being taught.

But then there are other candidates for the position of 'education in the true sense'. Michael Oakeshott, for instance, an eloquent writer on educational-philosophical topics, maintains that true education is necessarily unconcerned with goals other than those internal to itself. True education is an intrinsic good, and has regard only to the intrinsic worth of its subject matter. If anyone is educated *for* something else, for the priesthood, or for medicine, teaching or industry, then what this person is experiencing, whatever he may think of the matter, is not true education but something else. (See 'Education: the Engagement and its Frustration', in *Education and the Development of Reason*, edited by R. F. Dearden, P. Hirst and R. S. Peters, Routledge and Kegan Paul, 1972.) Since we do, all of us, speak of medical education, legal education and education as a tool to be used in various non-educational contexts, it will be obvious why Oakeshott, too, has to have recourse to the notion of 'true' education, as opposed to false; education properly, as opposed to improperly, so-called.

Again, if, as is sometimes maintained, the defining aim of education is to make people better, and if one could not say of a man that he was educated unless he was better than he had been before, how could one raise the question (which, after all, is sometimes raised) whether it is better for a man to be educated or not? Too rigid a definition appears to rule out certain questions altogether, but the trouble is that these may be the very questions which it is of practical importance to discuss, and to which, in realistic and political terms, we need answers. It is better, therefore, to be flexible about the concept of education, and not to insist that our first, or even our last, task is to define it exactly.

There are some respects in which education is like football. In the first place there are manifestly many different kinds of football, and according to our preference or our upbringing, we may be inclined to call some versions of the game more real or proper, more 'true', than others. But also the word 'football', as J. L. Austin taught us about 'golf', is often used adjectivally, and when it is, the object so qualified may stand in a vast number of different relations to the game itself. (Compare, for instance, 'football boot', 'football crowd', 'football enthusiast', 'football metaphor'.) Now although education has its own separate adjective, 'educational', still the relation to education of the things described as educational may be as various as the relation to football of the things described by the adjective 'football'. The use of the adjectives over a wide field, Austin argued, does not prove that there is a single simple quality, *educationality*, or *footballhood*, which is referred to in all the uses, or which gives them their sense. There is no mysterious unanalysable essence either of education or of football for which we must search. In both cases alike we can start, and finish, with the multiplicity of intelligible uses of the term.

In another respect, too, education and football might be thought parallel. One could work out a case for studying the philosophy of football, and could construct a syllabus quite as far-ranging and interesting as the average syllabus on the philosophy of education. The technique would be to pick out those questions in the contemporary philosophers' repertoire which could be deployed without too much distortion, and to apply them to aspects of football in the widest sense. This would be what R. S. Peters, that tireless spinner of the fabric of educational philosophy, refers to as 'the application of existing work to a new context' (Introduction to *The Philosophy of Education*, edited by R. S. Peters, Oxford Readings in Philosophy, 1973). Thus, in a collected volume of essays in football philosophy, you might find a discussion of the concept of a game in general; there would be room for a discussion of rules; of authority, as manifested in the referee, or the body responsible for the making and revising of rules. Justice or fairness in decision-making could be analysed, and there could be a search for the foundation of value judgements, exemplified either in spectator judgements as to the beauty or skill of a certain bit of play, or in the participants' assessments that this or that strategy would be better. All this could be perfectly seriously undertaken, and, given the central position of football in daily life, perhaps it should be.

But I believe that despite these similarities, the case with the philosophy of education is rather different. It might be interesting, and perhaps conducive to clarity of thought, to analyse the concepts which we employ in talking about or in playing football. But it does not greatly matter if we prefer simply to enjoy football and not bother with the philosophy. Our enjoyment will probably not be any the less, nor will our lives be impoverished. If it comes to that, we may prefer to have nothing whatever to do with football, and take no interest in it, and we shall be none the worse. But the effect on us and our society of education is dynamic. Its function is to turn children into a special sort of grown-up, namely an educated grown-up. So how this is done, with what in mind it is done, how much money we are to spend on it, how a choice is to be made as to what is taught, are all of them questions of urgent and practical importance. It is the theory behind *these* questions, questions which have to be answered in one way or another, that I believe to compose the philosophy of education. Such philosophy may well, from time to time, look rather like the putative philosophy of football. We may be compelled to raise quite general questions about the nature of authority or of knowledge itself, since these are the concepts which will inevitably enter into our practical conclusions. But the difference between this and the football philosophy is that questions about education *have* to be raised. They are not optional. In this respect they are not merely *like* political and moral questions, they *are* political and moral questions. This is because the answers to them will affect the way we live, even if only at several removes, or in a remote future.

Plato is often thought of as the first practitioner of the philosophy of education, and with justice. Many of the central topics in our subject first appear in his dialogues, though some of them were doubtless raised before that by the historical Socrates. Thus, as we shall see in due course, the question whether virtue can be taught, undoubtedly a Socratic question, is still one of the main problems in educational philosophy. But, leaving aside the distinction between historical Socratic problems and others, if we consider a central example of Plato's thought, his *Republic*, we can see clearly the respects in which the philosophy of education is different from the philosophy of football, or indeed of any other gratuitous subject matter. Although we may feel that almost all the doctrines which Plato presented in the *Republic* are, as far as education goes, either politically objectionable or manifestly false, or both, the book remains central in the history of the subject, because of the kinds of problems to which its doctrines are presented as solutions.

I shall return to the *Republic* in Chapter III of the present book; but I want to consider it here in a preliminary and quite general way. The reason why Plato was so much interested in education was because he believed that the content of the educational curriculum had a profound, direct and irreversible effect upon those who followed it. This seems less clear and simple to us than it did to him. Nevertheless, if we did not think that it had *some* effect we should presumably worry less than we do about how curricula should be constructed, and what syllabuses should contain. In this regard, it is doubtless the simplicity of Plato's views which distinguish him from us. For instance, no one would now hold, I suppose, that those who study history or Homer, or, say, the Old Testament, are bound to become like the heroes in the works they study. Nor would anyone hold that acting the part of a bad man on the stage was necessarily damaging to the actor. We distinguish between truth and fiction (or, for that matter, falsehood and fiction); between style and content; between a vision or picture of reality and reality itself, in a way that Plato did not. But the crucial thing is that Plato held it to be manifestly obvious that, since educational curricula had an effect on those who followed them, then in an ideal state the content of these curricula would be controlled by the state. If the curriculum which was traditionally accepted were good it would be adopted. If it were bad it would be dispensed with, in the ideal state. Homer would be suitably cut. A bad curriculum was one which caused those who followed it to become bad. It would be improved, when it had to be, by direct legislative action from above. And a good curriculum would then produce good people.

Plato's general theory seems to have been that a man becomes good by exposure to good in his environment. So the whole purpose of education is to induce in a man the taste or appetite for the good, by a process of habituation. This general theory, doubtless modified a bit, is held unquestioningly by many people today, and it is liable to various criticisms. But I want to concentrate on just one consequence of the general view. Granted that education, according to this theory, involves distinguishing between what is good in the environment and what is bad, then someone has to have authority to make this distinction. According to Plato, the decision as to what is good is made, not by the educators, nor, of course, by those who are being educated, but by the government, in the person of the philosopher-kings. The government is uniquely able, he thought, to claim knowledge of right and wrong, good and evil, just and unjust, or would be so in an ideal state. Those chosen to govern in the ideal state would be genetically superior to the members of the state who would be subject to them, and moreover they would have been educated, themselves, in a far more rigorous and long-drawn-out school. It would be for these reasons that they would have come to see what is good and what bad. Their right to rule would indeed be dependent on the fact that they, and they only, could make this distinction.

Now these ideal rulers would govern the state not for their own sakes, to make things better for themselves, nor because they would enjoy power. Personally, indeed, they would be the losers. They would prefer to pursue their education still further, and devote themselves entirely to mathematics and philosophy. But they would take on the burden of government and administration altruistically, for the sake of the common good, for the state itself. So the education they lay down for others would be designed to benefit the state as a whole. The question whether a particular man might prefer to learn or to teach something else, might see some advantage or pleasure in studying the vulgar as well as the elevated bits of Homer, would not be in any way a serious consideration. What he learns or teaches is determined by what the state needs people to teach and learn. This may sound at first like a thoroughly relativist position. It sounds as if whatever the state *deems* to be good or useful, for the time being, is sold to people under the title 'good', as a way of making them accept it (a cynical, or Hobbesean position). But in fact Plato's view is neither cynical nor relativist. On the contrary: there is supposed to be one permanent and immutable answer to the question 'What things are good?' But this answer will always be such that whatever is good is so for the state as a whole; and the knowledge that this is the case, as well as the knowledge of what it is that *is* good, is in the possession of the government. For Plato, then, there is genuinely no difference between educational and political criteria for deciding what should be taught. And the same is true if the question is to whom it is to be taught. An educationally good school would for him also be a politically desirable school. He would have no way of drawing a distinction between the two standards.

Now Plato is commonly criticized for this kind of view. It is said that one of the things that has gone wrong with education at the present time is that political considerations have entered where they have no place. And regrettably it is hard altogether to deny the force of this. But those who complain tend to assume that there is a set of purely educational arguments about what should be taught and to whom, which are perfectly distinct from any arguments about the needs of the state or about what would be politically desirable. This assumption needs to be examined, and it is part of my purpose in the following pages to conduct the examination.

More than a hundred years ago John Stuart Mill argued that if politicians were in a position to determine curricula in schools they would certainly do so; and that if they did, it would be an unmitigated evil; 'A general State education is a mere contrivance for moulding people to be exactly like one another: and as the mould in which it casts them is that which pleases the predominant power in the government, whether this be a monarch, a priesthood, an aristocracy or the majority of the existing generation; in proportion as it is efficient and successful, it establishes a despotism over the mind, leading by natural tendency to one over the body.' (J. S. Mill, *On Liberty*, Chapter V.) Yet in the same chapter he also argues that the state must declare its interest in education as an undoubted good for its citizens. It should enforce education by law, and even set up a universal examining system for the maintenance of educational standards. So while Mill seems to assume that there should be total freedom for individuals to determine, on purely educational grounds, what their children should be taught, he also assumes that a government ought to ensure a certain amount of education for everyone as a right. 'Is it not almost a self-evident axiom that the State should require and compel the education, up to a certain standard, of every human being who is born its citizen?' (*Op. cit.*) The two parts of Mill's argument are not contradictory. It is perfectly possible to use them both together as he does. But as soon as one begins to wonder, as one must, what is meant by 'up to a certain standard', then difficulties begin to appear. Who determines the standard? What do they have in mind in determining it? Is the standard to be the same for everyone? Have children any right to be educated beyond a minimum? Does an identical standard mean identical curricula for all children? It is in answering such questions as these that the absolute distinction between educational and political criteria, implied by Mill, may become difficult to maintain.

I want in the following pages to begin to explore the extent of the political component in educational decisions. Are there any *purely* educational criteria for deciding what education should be like? What sorts of arguments are used when people argue for or against some practice on educational or academic grounds? If sometimes such arguments turn out to have a high moral component, if, for instance, it is said that *all* children *ought* to be taught this or that because their lives will be better, then I believe that we should not be too much surprised or horrified. In any case it would be better to face facts and recognize that our educational judgements very often commit us morally, and hence, potentially, politically also. This is, of course, the very reason why everyone, and not just the educationalists, should make educational judgements. For even if we may, in part, agree with Plato that decisions about education are, or may be, also political, yet we may profoundly disagree with him about who should make such decisions. That they are political would be a sufficient reason to deny that only politicians should make them.

There is one further reason for hoping for a wider interest in educational philosophy. At present there sometimes seems to be a vast gap between practitioners of education and theorists. The result of this is that either theories devised in universities get delivered to practising teachers in schools, from above, like god-given laws, or they never get divulged at all. These faults are, in a way, opposites, and both are bad. On the one hand, good research may go to waste, or be done over and over again through bad dissemination. On the other hand, exciting ideas may become simplified into dogmas, when they were never meant to be more than bright suggestions, to be confirmed or disproved by practice. Instead they may come to dictate practice, not necessarily with good results. Such faults could be largely overcome if the connexions between theory and practice were seen to be closer, and if at the same time, everyone involved in practice were also, as a matter of course, familiar with, and indeed consciously contributing to, the development of theory.

This is, in my view, how educational philosophy should be justified. There is no reason to believe that philosophy would cease to be philosophy if it had consequences. (An interesting, more fully worked-out view of the relation between philosophy and practice in education is to be found in a recent collection of essays from the School of Education at Liverpool University: *Theory and the Practice of Education*, edited by A. Hartnett and M. Naish, 2 volumes, Heinemann, 1976.)

I

The Distribution of Education

My aim, then, is to cast some light, if possible, on the relation
between education and politics.

A political concept which has most obviously had life, perhaps even a life of its own, in the context of education during
the whole of this century is the concept of equality. I want to
treat this as the test case, the supreme example, of a political
notion, in order to see whether by itself it can dictate any solutions to educational problems.

I must make a preliminary and provisional distinction between
the distribution and the content of education. This distinction,
as we shall see, is in fact somewhat artificial; it becomes difficult
to discuss one without finding oneself discussing the other at the
same time. And the risk is, always, of turning the discussion into
something hopelessly abstract.

Starting with the problem of distribution, one can see how
this risk arises. The subject is relatively manageable if one is
prepared to treat education like cake or wealth, as a commodity
which can be handed out to people in greater or lesser amounts,
and which they are presumed to want. But there are serious
objections to regarding education in this light, and it is doing so
which tends to make the discussion of distribution unrealistic. I
shall have something to say about this later in the chapter. For
the time being, however, having acknowledged that there are
difficulties, I would like to proceed as if education could be so
regarded, and to consider some kinds of arguments used about
educational distribution on this assumption.

It is notoriously hard to distinguish the concept of equality from that of justice (or fairness). And both, oddly, are closely linked to the notions of compassion, pity and a sense of the brotherhood of man. This last connexion is at first sight surprising, because in other contexts one is in the habit of *contrasting* justice with mercy or compassion, justice being supposed to deal evenly and according to a strict rule of what is due, or what is deserved, while mercy does not look to dues or rights, but only to the humanity or capacity for suffering of the recipients of the hand-out, perhaps thinking more of their needs than their entitlements. But when on the other hand, in the context of education, the argument turns on equality of distribution, such equality is often linked with, and indeed thought to entail, special treatment for those who are least privileged; and this is in turn linked with 'compassion' or 'caring' for the under-privileged. In consequence, those who are sceptical about equality tend to emerge from the argument looking like hard-hearted indifferent graspers, while those who wish to use the principle of equality come out looking 'concerned', 'compassionate' and in favour of the brotherhood of all mankind. It is essential to steer carefully among these various confusions.

But let us return for the time being to the twin notions of equality and justice. It is the general demand of justice that where there is a rule governing people's behaviour, whether a rule for the distribution of goods or of some other kind, the rule should apply universally. This is probably a tautology. For if there were some groups of people to whom the rule did not apply then these people would not be governed by the same rule (there might of course be people who were *exceptions* to a rule, but treating them as exceptions would still be treating them in accordance with the rule under which they were exceptions). We may try to make this clearer by means of the kind of illustration used by Robert Nozick in his book *Anarchy, State and Utopia* (Blackwell, 1974). If there are two sets of people on two different planets, whose behaviour in no way overlaps, who are pursuing different goals and aiming at different things, then as far as the other planet goes, each planet is entirely free to do as it likes. The people on each planet may be governed by a rule, but unless there is some overlap in their interests, they cannot be said to be governed by the same rule. So the question of this rule's applying to all the people on both planets does not arise. Suppose that on one planet things are very bad. Resources are limited, people are unhappy, their lives miserable and inefficient, while on the other planet things are extremely good. Now in these circumstances, we could argue that, in an absolute sense, things would be better if life on the miserable planet were to be improved; but we could not say that it would be fairer or more just if this were to be done, because there is no sense in which the people on the two planets are in competition with one another, or in which they can even be legitimately compared. If we *do* compare them, we have to introduce a common standard by which to bring one planet into relation with the other, and this standard *ex hypothesi* is not a standard which *they* can use. For their interests and aims are entirely different, and therefore their standards are different. (In a somewhat similar way it would be absurd to speak of injustice in distribution between men and other animals on the same planet. There are obvious instances of men treating animals badly, starving them, neglecting them, and so on, or killing too many of them for their own pleasure. But though such things may be *bad* they cannot be described as unfair, unless the animals are by courtesy thought of as governed in their behaviour by the same rules as the people.) The question of justice between the planets cannot arise until a rule is envisaged which is to apply to both. The moment such a rule *is* envisaged, then it must apply to both planets and not to one alone.

But of course to say that a rule must apply to everyone alike is not yet to say that the effect of the application of the rule shall be the same for everyone. Obviously, for example, a law forbidding the use of tobacco could apply to everyone in a particular country equally; but it would not affect a non-smoker in the same manner as it would affect someone who, before the rule was enacted, had been smoking forty cigarettes a day. There is nothing unjust in this. It simply is so. To take a case familiar enough in theories, if not in life, suppose that there is a

23

number of hungry people and a cake. It is good and sensible to distribute the cake among the hungry people. It makes things better for people and therefore in a straightforward way it is a good thing to do. But I do not think it is yet a *just* thing to do. Justice comes in at the moment when we say 'there is a rule that the cake shall be distributed among the people'; and to say this involves taking a practical political decision. When that decision is taken, rights are created among everyone present to a share of the cake. If, before the political decision, we are inclined to speak of the 'natural justice' of distributing the cake, we should acknowledge that we can justify this concept in turn only by reference to 'natural law' which lays down that in a situation of scarcity, everyone ought to have some cake if a cake exists, or alternatively that everyone has a natural right to a piece of cake. But we should acknowledge also that speaking in these terms is not exactly to say that there *is* a right which could be proved, but only that there ought to be. If we speak of natural justice, natural laws, or natural rights we are in fact speaking in terms of our own moral standards; we are saying in persuasive language that we think things would be better if the cake were to be distributed. The language is persuasive just because it is borrowed from the political situation in which an actual law has been decided upon.

When the political decision *has* been taken, and the right to a piece of cake has thereby been created, this right is an equal right. Everyone present has an equal right to a piece of cake, and no one's right may justly be neglected in favour of another's (nor indeed simply neglected, in nobody's favour). Everyone counts for one. But though under the newly made rule everyone has a right to some of the cake, so far the rule has not specified how the cake shall be distributed. All we have established is that, in justice, everyone has an equal right to a bit of cake.

But now we may imagine that the rule is made specific on the point of how the cake is to be distributed. It may lay down that everyone shall have a piece of cake of the same size, or it may devise some way of proportioning the size of the piece to the person, either matching size for size, or inventing a way of measuring greater hunger, greater need, or greater possible output of goods in return for a piece of cake. So, for instance, there could be a simple rule which laid down that men had twice as much as women, women twice as much as children. Or there could be a rule that those who had done some particularly demanding or useful work in the past had two slices. Absolutely any principle capable of being expressed could feature as the principle of distribution. And under whatever principle was adopted, justice would demand that each person had an absolute right, not to be overridden, to whatever was laid down for him by the rule. No one should forego his right, such as it was. So far it is obvious that equality comes in only in so far as everyone equally has *a* right of some kind. To take another familiar example: if there is a law which lays down that everyone is entitled to what he has mixed his labour with, then I may be entitled to much less than my neighbour, because I am lazy and have mixed my labour with very little. All that justice demands is that the law should apply equally to me and my neighbour, with all the inequality of actual possession, or entitlement to possession, which that application will entail.

Now of course it is possible to criticize the original rule, and to argue, to go back to the first example, that discrimination between different hungry people on grounds of age or sex is wrong. It will often indeed be said to be unfair. But if it is said to be unfair, this must be on the basis of some different rule which, it is held, exists or ought to exist, and which is a morally better rule. To say that a rule would be morally better is to say that it pays attention to more important features of the situation. It might be argued, for instance, that being human is a more important thing than being male or female or ten years old, and that therefore a rule of distribution should pay attention only to this feature of the competing potential cake-receivers. On this basis it would be argued that everyone human should receive the same amount as everyone else human. There is no difference, it would be said, among the possible recipients sufficiently important to outweigh this common feature. But on this rule, the dogs and cats will perhaps have to go hungry. The salient point

25

is that the rule itself has to specify that every human being must get the same amount in virtue of his humanity, otherwise there is no necessary or intrinsic injustice in people getting different amounts from one another. One needs a special argument, a special clause in the rule, to ensure that the equal application of the rule to all will result in everyone's getting the same amount. To write in such a special clause will of course be a further and more complicated political decision. It will be a decision of value—that, for instance, size is to be deemed irrelevant in the matter of distribution of cake to humans, or on the other hand past service to the community is to be counted as a relevant factor.

Applying these considerations, then, to the case of education, it will be seen that there is a difference between claiming that everyone has an equal right to education and saying that everyone has a right to equal education. In order to claim either of these rights it is necessary that there should be a law. But the law under which the second claim could be made would be a great deal more specific than the law under which the first could be made. It is the second claim, that everyone has a right to equal education, which is generally known as egalitarianism. But the first claim, that everyone has an equal right to education is itself a political claim, and cannot be upheld unless there is a law which makes it obligatory that people shall be educated. J. S. Mill, as we have seen (page 18), argued strongly in favour of what did not exist at the time, namely compulsory education for everyone in the country, but yet thought that the content and extent of the education should not be determined by law at all. He certainly would not, therefore, have argued in favour of a specific law laying down that everyone had a right to an equal education, whatever this might have meant.

This stronger claim, which we have called egalitarianism, is obviously the contentious claim at the present time. Before looking at its educational implications, it is perhaps worth considering egalitarianism in general, since a number of arguments tend to make use of the concept, ambiguous and uncertain though its boundaries are. There have been a good many attempts by philosophers to clarify the issues. For instance, the crucial distinction between the equal right to a share of some good and the right to an equal share of that good was clearly drawn and analysed by Richard Wollheim in the *Proceedings of the Aristotelian Society* (1956). Wollheim argues that, as we have seen already, if the first claim is made (that everyone has an equal right to a share) the result may be a gross difference between the shares of different parties, and this may be manifestly inequitable. That is to say, we may feel that the upshot is unfair. But he says, 'In all the cases of inequitable societies that claim to respect everyone's equal right to property, what is wrong with the claim is not a false interpretation of what it is for everyone to possess an equal right, but a false view of what right it is that anyone possesses.' He goes on to raise the question whether, since such inequitable results may follow from the doctrine that everyone has an equal right, the word 'equal' actually adds anything to the statement that everyone has rights. If the equality of the entitlement tells us nothing about what it is that each person is entitled to, then might one not just as well, and less misleadingly, simply say that everyone has the rights he has? However, he goes on to argue that in fact the doctrine of *equality* of rights has an important implication, which cannot be omitted from the statement of it. If we feel that the doctrine may by itself lead to a result which is inequitable, this is because in stating it, we are implicitly stating our demand that inequality in actual distribution must somehow be justified by a rule. 'In other words, the principle of equal rights demands that if two people have rights to different quantities of some commodity, then there must be some difference elsewhere that justifies this.' As we have seen, any principle of division with regard to differences among the recipients could be adopted; but there must be *some* principle. If people are genuinely to be held to possess equal rights, then if they end up with different amounts of the good to be distributed, one must be able to specify in virtue of what difference in *them* they are rightly the recipients of different amounts. But one must notice that, if a sense of unfairness is to be avoided, the principle of distribution must be a good one independently of its being equally applied. And the criterion of its goodness will not itself be that of equality; a concept other than that of equality itself is needed. This point is of the greatest importance.

Wollheim goes on to examine a rather different kind of situation, but one which may well have more relevance to our particular concerns. He considers competitive situations, in which all the competitors have equal rights, but not all can have what they want. Some would argue, he says, that we cannot *both* hold that everyone possesses equal rights in a certain field *and* allow that this is a proper field for competition, since competition and rights are incompatible. Now it is certainly true that competition and the right to *win* are logically incompatible; but competition and the right to compete are manifestly not. Wollheim discusses the philosopher's favourite example of the coin which is found on the pavement, in a legal situation in which anyone has a right to keep what they find and pick up. In this case anyone has a right to pick up and keep the coin, though only one person can do so. So, though A and B both have a right to try for the coin, A has no duty to allow B to have it, nor the other way round. There are no duties correlated to the rights. But, Wollheim argues, there is an important point here where morals and law part company. 'B has no duty correlative to A's right, that is to say he has no duty to let A do what he has a right to do, but his recognition of A's right does commit him to exercising some restraint upon his own conduct.' In the eyes of the moralist, though the mere fact of competition does not infringe the rights of other competitors, there are some ways of conducting the competition which would. If B used his superior eyesight to see the coin in the first place and his longer legs and greater dexterity to get to it and pick it up, A's right to pick up the coin would not have been infringed, whatever the outcome. But if B had actually tricked A into not seeing the coin, or if he had tripped him up or knocked him over on his way to getting it, then, though the result would be the same, the moralist would be outraged, and the competition would be held to be unfair. Now Wollheim, I think rightly, concludes from this that morally there are restraints on conduct which *ought* to be applied in competitions. But he also concludes that in order to decide what these retraints are one has to look at each situation separately. There are no *a priori* means of determining how people should behave in order to avoid what will be felt to be unfair. So once again we have reached the position in which we can see that some *other* principle, not merely that of equality of rights, is necessary in order that the idea of fairness or a good outcome shall be satisfied. In two different ways, and from two different directions, Wollheim has argued that the 'principle of equality' is not sufficient by itself to satisfy our demand for fairness. When applied to the case of education, this theoretical point turns out to be of the greatest consequence.

There is, however, one more perfectly general argument about equality which must be looked at, since it is very often adduced as relevant to education, albeit confusedly. The argument is set out and discussed by Isaiah Berlin in an article on equality which follows the discussion by Wollheim (*Proceedings of the Aristotelian Society*, 1956). Roughly speaking, it runs as follows: Strict egalitarians really, whatever they claim, must want everyone to be exactly alike. But people are not exactly alike, nor should we like it if they were; therefore egalitarianism is not to be taken seriously since it can be shown to aim at an unwelcome impossibility. Berlin himself does not take this short way with the egalitarians. But his discussion of the claims of egalitarians shows how one may be tempted into it. My contention is that egalitarianism is to be taken seriously and no short way is possible. It is for this reason that I think it desirable to consider exactly what egalitarianism does demand.

Berlin agrees that, as we have seen, the application of equality of distribution depends on the existence of some set of rules according to which the distribution is to be made, and to which everyone is equally subject. Now some people, he suggests, object to this because they object to rules as such. This is to attack the very ideal of social equality in any form. So what is this ideal? 'In its simplest form the ideal of complete social equality embodies the wish that everything and everybody should be as similar as possible to everything and everybody else.' The egalitarian will object to any inequality of distribution unless a sufficient reason can be produced; and he will be extremely critical of what is to count as a sufficient reason for inequality in outcome. Berlin says, 'Even the most convinced social egalitarian does not normally object to the authority wielded by, let us say, the conductor of an orchestra. Yet there is no obvious reason why he should not. . . . Those who maintain that equality is the paramount good may not wish to be fobbed off with the explanation that the purpose of orchestral playing will not be served if every player is allowed equal authority with the conductor in deciding what is to be done. . . . A fanatical egalitarian could maintain that the inequality of the players in relation to the conductor is a greater evil than a poor performance of a symphonic work, and that it is better that no symphonic music be played at all if a conductorless orchestra is not feasible, than that such an institution should be allowed to offend against the principle of equality.' He sums up as follows: 'So long as there are differences between men some degree of inequality may occur.' And one should add so long as there are differences among the roles men play in various institutions, some inequalities will occur, and be fixed as part of the institution. But 'there is no kind of inequality against which a pure egalitarian may not be moved to protest simply on the grounds that he sees no reason for tolerating it, no argument that seems more powerful than the argument for equality itself'. Berlin does not think that anyone has ever consciously argued for this pure and fanatical version of egalitarianism; but he does think, rightly, that all demands for greater equality, that is to say, all complaints which have been brought against the inequalities tolerated in any field, have all been modifications of this absolute ideal which 'therefore possesses the central importance of an ideal limit or idealized model at the heart of all egalitarian thought'.

Now the suggestion is sometimes made, and not least in the field of education, that if the nature of this central ideal is made plain, if the simplified model is brought out into the open and shown up as entailing the absurd demand that everyone should be the same as everyone else (that nothing shall be counted as a legitimate reason for differentiating between one person and another) then that will be the end of egalitarianism. If there is an absurdity in the central ideal, it is argued, then when this is exposed all arguments turning on a demand for equality will be instantly refuted. But this is not so. The quite general point is this: it is the function of an ideal to be unattainable. It is no argument against adopting an ideal, therefore, to show that it is impossible to attain it. But, more important, if it is shown that an ideal pursued to the exclusion of all others would have undesirable consequences, this is no argument against it either. For we are not, morally speaking, committed to just one ideal; nor are all our ideals necessarily compatible one with another. Berlin himself sums up as follows: 'Equality is one value among many: the degree to which it is compatible with other ends depends on the concrete situation, and cannot be deduced from general laws of any kind; it is neither more nor less rational than any other ultimate principle.' We value a whole number of different things, and if they can be shown to conflict with one another, this is not to prove that we never really valued them. What it does suggest is that not all problems in morality, or in any other field in which values are going to determine our decisions, are soluble; or rather, not all problems have one best or correct solution. As soon as we recognize that more than one value is involved, we realize that we may well have to compromise, and come up with a solution which is not bad, while not being ideal. For the ideal, *ex hypothesi* cannot, in such a situation of conflict, be arrived at.

Such generalities, indeed platitudes, turn out in practical and political situations to be very important. But theoretically as well it seems to me worth emphasizing that it is not a sufficient reason for rejecting a value that it should be shown to be in conflict with another, also accepted, value. And those many who frivolously say, 'How dull life would be if the uniformity entailed in egalitarianism were to be achieved', or who, more pedantically, say, 'how impossible it is that the similarity between people entailed by egalitarianism should exist', have neither of them produced an argument against egalitarianism. If there are arguments to be adduced, and I am sure that there are, they must be on the grounds that some more important ideal may be in danger if the egalitarian ideal is allowed to become too dominant. But in order to consider such arguments we are obliged to consider how equality conflicts, if it does, with other principles by which we determine what is good.

It is now time to turn back to where we started and consider the application of egalitarianism to educational theory. So far the discussion has all turned on the idea of equality in the distribution of some stuff, whether cake or wealth. Wollheim, it is true, in his argument, did use the example of competition, and of equality in the power to change legislation, and Berlin the example of equality in authority; but these examples were assimilated to that of the desirable *stuff*, cake or money, to be handed out. We deliberately started with the assumption that education was of that kind.

But there are difficulties. For a start, if I am given a piece of cake and you are given another, we are in an easy sense given the same stuff. I may eat my piece and you may feed yours to the ducks or crumble it on to the floor. But the use we make of the cake is not relevant to the question of what we were given in the first place. But there are those who would want to argue that if a child is offered an education which he *cannot* make use of then he has not been offered the same thing as has been offered to one who can and does make use of it. According to this way of looking at the matter, education is something which happens to a child and changes him for the better. So if a child is not changed for the better, what he has had is not education. Thus the analogy of the hand-out of cake or money is totally misleading. Education is, it is said, *essentially* something which must be tailored to its recipient. What is distributed indifferently among a lot of recipients cannot be called education. Moreover, the very idea of handing education out is mistaken according to the contention of these theorists. For education must come from the pupil himself. He does not wait about with open hands to receive what is given him. On the contrary, he develops, grows, or realizes his potential. Education is growth: what educators have to do is make sure that this growth is not inhibited, or that it is, more positively, encouraged.

The notion of education as a species of growth has a long history. Rousseau certainly thought of education as properly connected with the natural development of the child, something which had therefore to occur *as* the child grew, and only with the active participation of the child. But R. F. Dearden suggests, probably rightly, that the biological or horticultural analogy underlying the use of the idea of growth in many non-philosophical writings about education is more derivative from Froebel than from Rousseau ('Education as a Process of Growth' in *Education and the Development of Reason*, edited by Dearden, Hirst and Peters, Routledge and Kegan Paul, 1972, p. 77). Dewey, on the other hand, thought of growth as a social phenomenon, and identified education with the provision of an environment in which social growth was possible. 'A society of free individuals in which all, through their own work, contribute to the liberation and enrichment of the lives of others is the only environment in which any individual can really grow normally to his full stature.' Such growth would come about by the provision of experiences of a growth-enhancing kind. 'Any experience is mis-educative that has the effect of arresting or distorting the growth of further experience. An experience may be such as to engender callousness; it may produce lack of sensitivity and responsiveness. Then the possibilities of having richer experience in the future are restricted.' (J. Dewey, *Experience and Education*, New York, 1938.) But, though no longer horticultural, the language here is still metaphorical. Dewey could not mean it literally when he says that only in a certain educational environment can an individual grow to his normal stature. This dependence upon metaphor is sometimes made explicit. For example Sidney Hook, disciple of Dewey, in an essay entitled 'The Ends and Content of Education' wrote as follows (in *Education and the Taming of Power*, Alcove Press, 1974): 'the conception of teaching as the pouring of the same stuff into passive containers expresses a point of view that is hard to reconcile with what we know about children as organic creatures and learners whose differential responses determine how much they can assimilate. It would help to change our metaphors. Our . . . task is to find and offer the appropriate curricular nourishment for different types of organisms that will enable them to achieve the full measure of their growth and health.' Whatever the source of the concept of education as growth and however biological or otherwise its metaphors are, there is no doubt that it has been for a long time now one of the ways in which people think of education. Section 2 of the Plowden Report (HMSO, 1967), for example, was concerned with the Growth of the Child. And in paragraph 505 it puts forward, as a main method of educational reform, 'deliberately to devise the right environment for children, to allow them to be themselves and to develop in the way and at the pace appropriate to them'. Now this way of thinking suggests that education must be the providing of opportunities; and therefore equality, if it is an educational goal, must in turn be thought of as equality of opportunity for all children to grow.

At the same time, there is another course of argument which has led in the same direction, namely towards the notion o. equality of educational *opportunity*. This argument has nothing to do with the theoretical nature of education. It is strictly practical. For it is observed that education, meaning what is on offer in schools and universities, is graded by its consumers as good and bad, high and low. Good education is traditionally associated with good jobs and high salaries (though this association may well be loosening at the present time); and, in general, specialist and university education has been thought to be available only for a relatively small number of people. (This fact has of course not been unconnected with the concept of some jobs as intrinsically 'superior', which *entails* that they are not available to everyone.) If education is looked on in this light, as, whatever else it is, in practice a ladder or set of stepping stones to a desirable goal which cannot be reached by everyone, then at once the notion of competition enters the field. So we have to go back to the idea of equality of right discussed by Wollheim (page 28). In a competition no one has a right to win, and not everyone can win, in the nature of the case. So the final outcome is not going to be that everyone has a prize (or the same amount of education). What the principle of equality demands on this view is that no one should be debarred from the right to *enter* the competition, a right to get on to the ladder if he can. So once again we end up talking about equality of opportunity rather than equality of education itself.

But equality of opportunity is by no means the rallying cry that once it was. Indeed it is, at the time of writing, a suspect if not positively out-dated notion. It is therefore necessary to consider in rather more detail whether it has in fact any use in the theory of education. At once we face a new set of difficulties, not the least of which is that the idea of equality of opportunity is particularly associated with the optimistic non-radical socialism of the 1940s. (And here we have a proof, if one were needed, of the impossibility of separating educational theory from politics.) For we have seen that to a certain extent it was educationalists themselves who shifted the discussion from equality of distribution of education to equality of opportunity for receiving it (or benefiting from it) on the ground that the very nature of education made it inappropriate to speak of it as a kind of uniform material like cake, to be handed out. And we have also seen that the second source of the introduction of the notion of opportunity was the perfectly ordinary thought that education is a privilege, like position, or indeed power, which cannot be enjoyed to the same extent by everyone. It seems to me extremely unlikely that this kind of view of education can ever be totally eliminated (I shall hope to demonstrate this a little further on). It is also absolutely obvious that, if thought of in this light, education at once becomes as much a central subject for politics as is power itself. And philosophers of education must therefore face the fact that they are concerned with politics (which means among other things that they may find themselves lined up with particular people and particular policies which

35

may actually succeed or fail, be popular or unpopular, an un-familiar position for philosophers to be in).

We have seen that equality of opportunity involves the idea of competition. In his article 'The Idea of Equality' (originally in *Philosophy, Politics and Society*, 2nd series, edited by P. Laslett and W. G. Runciman, Blackwell, 1962, and reprinted in *Moral Concepts*, edited by Joel Feinberg, Oxford Readings in Philosophy, 1962), Bernard Williams explores this connexion further. He distinguishes between two sorts of inequality which may exist in the people to whom a distribution of any kind is to be made, inequality of need and inequality of merit. 'In the case of needs, such as the need for medical treatment in case of illness, it can be presumed for practical purposes that the persons who have the need actually desire the goods in question, and so the question can indeed be regarded as one of distribution in a simple sense. In the case of merit . . . there is not the same presumption that everyone who has the merit has the desire for the goods in question. . . . Moreover the good may be legitimately, if hopelessly, desired by those who do not possess the merit. . . . Hence the distribution of goods according to merit has a competitive aspect lacking in the case of distribution according to need. For this reason it is appropriate to speak in the case of merit not only of the distribution of the good, but of the distribution *of the opportunity of achieving* the good.' And this, Williams says, can be distributed equally though the good itself cannot.

There are two points to notice about this argument. First, the introduction of the concept of merit is important. For if one says that one person has more merit than another this is to make a value judgement albeit of limited scope, with regard to the people. Now perhaps one of the most popular injunctions to be selected from among Christian exhortations at the present time is the injunction 'judge not'; and the reason why people on the whole dislike either judging or being judged is a mixture of relativism and egalitarianism. I shall have more to say about relativism later. But, for the moment concentrating on the egalitarian argument, the suggestion that one person may deserve more than another, on merit, seems to many to offend against the deepest principles of humane toleration or charity. Although in ordinary conversation we may quite happily speak of people 'earning' or 'deserving' some good which they have acquired, and although, oddly, we may sometimes speak of people 'deserving' good fortune (which *ex hypothesi* can have befallen them only by chance, and so they cannot have been awarded it as a consequence of merit except on a very implausible idea of natural rewards and punishments), yet wherever the idea of 'desert' or 'merit' comes in for close examination, it tends to give rise to uneasiness. Ought children at school to be awarded prizes which they have deserved? Ought undergraduates at university to be classified according to merit? Does success in a competition ever reflect real merit? And if it does, ought such merit to be publicized, suggesting as it does that some people are *less* meritorious than others? All these questions are familiar enough, and they are at least partly responsible for the uneasiness felt about judging people according to merit. Somehow everyone ought to merit the same, since all are human, and all humans in *some* sense deserve the same treatment, merely in virtue of their humanity.

Secondly, we must not be lulled into supposing that we can understand precisely what is meant by equality of opportunity. If two people are both approaching the philosopher's coin on the pavement, and neither unfairly inhibits or distracts the other, then both presumably have the opportunity to pick it up. But only one of them can actually take possession of the coin. How can we be absolutely certain that the one who does not in the end come away with the coin actually had the opportunity to pick it up? He did not, we might say, make use of the opportunity he had. He did not seize it. But perhaps he was naturally very slow. He might surely say, 'I had no chance of getting the coin. X is so much quicker, and I am so stiff.' But 'chance' and 'opportunity' are not the same. Opportunity seems to be connected rather with some external features of the environment, some features of the situation in general, while chance is more closely related to the internal features of the protagonists themselves. The man who complains that he was too slow to have a chance is not complaining about his opportunities so much as about his fate (or perhaps his lack of practice, which might be caused by lack of opportunity to practise). I do not think, of myself, that I lacked the *opportunity* to be a solo violinist, but I certainly had no *chance* of becoming one, since I lacked the gifts or talent. There was however nothing about my environment or upbringing which prevented my becoming a violinist. However there is no absolute distinction between what we think of as 'external' and what as 'internal' features of a situation. And, as Bernard Williams points out (*Op. cit.*), more and more things about a man tend to be thought of as alterable features of his environment (external features). If it were to be discovered that the application of a certain discipline combined, let us say, with a particular diet, could produce a vast increase in musical talent, and if I had not had the discipline or the diet, though in some sense I might have had it (i.e. it had already been discovered at the appropriate period) then I might say that I had had no opportunity to become a violinist. The case would be like the case of a child who, though manifestly musical, lacks money to buy a violin or engage a teacher. The difficulty here is that we do not really know what features of people are changeable, what conditions are reversible, nor do we know how tolerable we would think it if great 'internal' change were regularly undertaken. Would society consider it reasonable to offer plastic surgery, for instance, to ugly children, so that they might have an opportunity to compete in Miss World competitions or become photographic models? Is the objection to such a suggestion merely financial? Or is it that the end, in this example, is a frivolous or unworthy end? Bernard Williams, in noticing these difficulties, concludes: 'A system of allocation will fall short of equality of opportunity if the allocation of the good in question in fact works out unequally or disproportionately between different sections of society, if the unsuccessful sections are under a disadvantage which could be removed by further reform or social action.' And he adds that if everything about a person, all his characteristics, were controllable, then equality of opportunity and absolute equality of persons would coincide.

We could in principle change everything about a man so that he would be in all relevant respects (all respects, that is, relevant to the competition in question) the same as those against whom he was competing. It seems obvious that there is more than mere practical or financial difficulty in the way of accepting such a possibility. The deeper objection we feel is something to do with human freedom, in turn connected closely with human individuality.

But it is perhaps time to turn from fantasy to consider some of the concrete difficulties that have arisen in an attempt to ensure equality of opportunity in education, difficulties which have proved so great that the notion of opportunity itself has had to be more or less expunged from educational thinking. Equality of educational opportunity was undoubtedly the goal of the 1944 Education Act. Much has been written about the theoretical assumptions of the Act. A short and useful discussion of some of the issues is to be found in the introduction to Maurice Kogan's *The Politics of Education* (Penguin, 1971), a more detailed account in *Equal Opportunity in Education*, a reader edited by H. Silver (Methuen, 1973). It is clear that the purpose of the Act was to ensure that everyone got the education he deserved. Schools were distinguished from each other on the basis of catering for the more or less academic who were, as individuals, sorted out by means of an examination at eleven, designed to test intelligence rather than knowledge. The gradual revulsion of feeling against the eleven-plus examination was concomitant with, perhaps partly productive of, the revision of the theory of equality of opportunity.

It has never been entirely clear what the equal opportunity at one time accepted as the goal of educational policy was opportunity *for*. 'Educational opportunity' is an ambiguous expression, for sometimes it could refer to opportunity for education, sometimes to opportunity for jobs, prestige, wealth, opportunities, that is, in life as a whole, in so far as these seemed to stem from having received education. In the early part of this century, the battle was still being waged to secure equal opportunity for education, secondary education, for everyone. And this really meant moving to the position that everyone should be entitled, not to the *chance* to be educated, but to the education itself. In 1922 R. H. Tawney in his pamphlet *Secondary Education for All* described three different views of secondary education. The first view, which he called the doctrine of separation, was roughly that the poor should receive elementary education, and nothing else, while the rich received secondary or higher education as a matter of course. This view was never seriously maintained in the twentieth century, though Tawney was doubtless right to say that at the time when he wrote 'its evil legacy was not yet exhausted'. The second view, which had by the twenties more or less completely replaced the first, was the doctrine of selection or the educational ladder, according to which children could win their right to secondary education by their abilities. The third view, for which he was arguing, was the doctrine of the single system, according to which all children proceeded from primary to secondary education, as of right. Nine years later, Tawney was arguing that if such entitlement were recognized, that is, if there were genuine equality of opportunity for secondary education, then in fact the consequence would be the end of the ladder view of education. 'The goal', he wrote, 'is simplicity itself. The primary school, as the Consultative Committee of the Board of Education asserted in its report on the subject, should be "the common school of the whole population, so excellent and so generally esteemed that all parents desire their children to attend it". It should in short be the preparatory school, from which all children, and not merely a fortunate minority, pass on to secondary education, and which since the second stage would then succeed the first as a matter of course when the children were ripe for it, would be free from the present pressure to prepare them for a competitive examination affecting their whole future.' We know now that although his vision of the common primary schools is largely realized, the end of the ladder view of education is not as straightforward as he thought. Equality of education does not necessarily follow from equality of opportunity to receive education of some sort or other. By the time of the 1944 Education Act, the concept of some secondary education for everyone was totally accepted, and the old notion of elementary education dead, but nevertheless the equality of opportunity offered by the Act was the opportunity, now open to all children, to *compete for* the best education for which they could be selected. The ladder view was reinforced by a new system and a new vocabulary.

But 'good' and 'best' are of course manipulable words. And the perfectly genuine, but also comforting, theory underlying the introduction of the eleven-plus test was that if a child did not win the best in the competition, he did at any rate win what was best for *him*, since he was *ex hypothesi* not a winner, so the prize would not in any case have been suitable for him. Perhaps more than any other factor it was this apparent attempt to combine incompatible theories which ultimately brought the Act into disrepute. For it seems now to be the height of disingenuousness to combine the theory of competition, a theory which quite openly admits that there is a prize to be won by the competitors, with the theory that everyone is going to be provided with something according to his need. The argument seemed to be that if you did not win a grammar school place then you had not really needed it, that is, you could not have used it to advantage, whatever you might have thought at the time. Your Real Will was against it. No wonder that parents became more and more hostile to the eleven-plus test.

So even though secondary education for all had been achieved, the academic ladder remained, but it became a concept which was not to be tolerated in public policy any more than the social ladder, an equally real, but equally deplorable idea, to be mentioned if at all only to be reviled. There is here a manifest divorce between acceptable public policy and what many people privately think, which is likely, as any such divorce is, to create difficulties for practical politicians. It would be interesting to make an analysis of key areas in which avowed public morality seems to split off, of necessity, from private morality. It is likely that many of these splits would be connected somehow with competition. Who believes in charity, generosity, selflessness or even equality where there is a prize to be won, a sexual conquest to be achieved, a house to be bought? Yet all these virtues are generally acclaimed, and sincerely admired. In the particular case of education there is no doubt of the existence, and indeed of the stimulus, of the ladder concept, but no politician of either party could speak of it as other than disgraceful and ripe for abolition.

The history of ideas relating to educational equality is perhaps particularly interesting in that policy-making and theory have so manifestly gone together, whether the policies have been made by civil servants, royal commissions or ministers. Thus it is unusually easy to trace changes in presuppositions, or in ideology, often expounded in a thoroughly abstract way, but having practical results. It is not perhaps surprising that ministers of education should on the whole be relatively articulate. If they do not determine new ideas, they may often expound existing assumptions in an illuminating way. The pronouncements of one Minister of Education, Anthony Crosland, are especially well worth studying, since he was not only an educational reformer, but also himself both academic and articulate. Moreover he believed in discussing the theories which lay behind his measures with other academic and articulate people. Crosland's period of office was only two and a half years (January 1965 until August 1967), but before this his views on equality in education were clearly formulated and had become relatively well known. In 1961 he had written an article in *Encounter*, which was reprinted the next year as part of his book *The Conservative Enemy* (Cape, 1962). It was the ideas there formulated which he tried to put into practice in his period in office. Crosland noticed two trends in the recruitment and selection of 'the élite which runs the country'. First, there was an ever-increasing premium on educational and professional qualifications. More people sought and gained educational qualifications and it was increasingly difficult to get on without them. Meanwhile the educational élite thus marked off was becoming socially more broadly based. 'As the occupational pyramid has widened at the top, a higher proportion of top positions has become available to non-public school boys.' Many people,

Crosland said, would therefore argue that equality of opportunity had been substantially achieved. But he denied this. Ironically, he wrote, 'We satisfy the platonic idea by having a superior segregated educational élite, and the democratic idea by permitting access to it without regard to birth or wealth.'

There are, he suggested, two interpretations of equality of opportunity, the weak interpretation and the strong. In the weak sense, equality of opportunity means access to élitist education by means of intelligence, measured by IQ tests. Even on this interpretation, he argued, equality was not achieved. First, the existence of the public schools available only to those who can pay (and, he suggests, much better educationally than maintained schools), made nonsense of claims to equal opportunity. Secondly, within grammar schools, to which access was by intelligence test, how children actually fared, how long they stayed at school and how well they could expect to do while they were there, depended largely on social class.

But in any case the weak interpretation of equal opportunity had to be rejected. For it depended for its acceptability on the theory that measuring intelligence was measuring a permanent, fixed, inborn characteristic of people which rendered them for ever suitable or unsuitable for élitist education. 'We now know', he wrote, 'that measured intelligence is not a purely innate characteristic; it is at least partly an acquired one. With this knowledge the whole discussion of equal opportunity takes on a new aspect. . . . Once we admit that measured intelligence is even partially acquired and . . . that many of the environmental influences are susceptible to social action, we can see why the previous interpretation of equal opportunity was described as "weak". . . . The "strong" definition of equal opportunity is therefore that, subject to differences in heredity and infantile experience, every child should have the same opportunity for *acquiring* measured intelligence in so far as this can be controlled by social action.' (*Op. cit.*) Here we have the sense of equal opportunity analysed, as we have seen, by Bernard Williams in his 1962 article. Where will it end? Social engineering has become the prime necessity if equality is to exist in any satisfactory way.

43

Crosland wrote: 'The implications of the strong definition are that we should eliminate inadequate incomes and bad housing and carry through a major educational revolution so that parents will stimulate their children, and children will develop their intelligence by education to the age of at least seventeen.' And, 'Those who now speak of equal opportunity think of a ladder. As soon as we adopt, as of course we should, the strong interpretation, we see that the phrase takes on a rather evolutionary connotation. Its realization would entail an immensely high standard of universal provision. The emphasis shifts from individual mobility to the general standard.' There is a further implication. For Crosland conducted most of his argument on the assumption that equality of opportunity should mean equality of the opportunity *to become intelligent*. But he realized that this assumption was itself unduly élitist, suggested perhaps too old-fashioned a view of who was and who was not worth educating, or what education was really intended to do. Explicitly throughout the main part of his article he stated that part of the point of education was to provide a technically efficient body of people capable of governing the country, controlling industry and so on. 'Education is highly relevant to National Efficiency.' But in a footnote, he mentions another view. He suggests that there may be a certain injustice in singling out this one trait (intelligence) for exceptionally privileged treatment. 'The strongest of all definitions of equal opportunity would be that every child has an equal chance of developing his interests and personality regardless of measured intelligence; and that might mean giving more education to the subnormal than to the brilliant child.' This was a different theory of education altogether. Equal opportunity to be educated now meant something like equal opportunity to be happy. It was towards this that the 'strongest possible' interpretation tended.

Crosland was not alone in this extension of the notion of equality. For one thing, Edward Boyle, Crosland's predecessor as Minister, had borrowed his words and incorporated them in the foreword to the Newsom Report of 1963. 'The essential point is that all children should have an equal opportunity of acquiring intelligence *and* developing their talents and abilities to the full.' Then the notion of social engineering to bring up the standard of the disadvantaged to an acceptable norm became current orthodoxy after the publication of the Plowden Report on Primary Education in 1967. It was there that the phrase 'positive discrimination' first appeared. In the fifth chapter of the report there is to be found the recommendation that *educational priority areas* should be designated, which should have special treatment with regard to school buildings and staffing ratios, in which, in general, the social services should concentrate their efforts to improve the lot of the total community from which the children come to the schools. The ladder conception of opportunity has certainly been almost entirely removed from this kind of recommendation. Although the Plowden Report was not specifically concerned with the subnormal or otherwise handicapped child, a great deal of the literature which is so concerned demonstrates the same assumptions. Equality of opportunity means an equal chance for *any* child, however handicapped at the start by social, physical or intellectual disadvantages, to 'develop to the full'. But once the notion of equal chances has spread out as broadly as this, it is very difficult to see how it can have any very specific bearing on education. When Crosland first wrote his article, and before he added the footnote, at least equal opportunity meant, as we have seen that it always tends to mean, an equal opportunity to compete in the same race as everyone else was competing in; an equal chance to get a foot on the same old ladder. And Crosland with his talk of the 'élite who run the country' does seem much of the time to subscribe, albeit reluctantly, to the ladder view. But of course it is in fact impossible to *make* everyone capable of competing in the race or even beginning to ascend the ladder. For one thing removing bad housing, low incomes and so on is an immense and probably endless task. But secondly it is not perhaps as certain as it seemed in the optimism of the sixties that, even if it could be done, the results would be dramatic. In the meantime it is easy to argue that what positive discrimination entails is a lessening of opportunities for those who are not disadvantaged, rather than any positive gain for those who are. Thus the *Daily Telegraph*, predictably enough, reacted fiercely to the Plowden Report. (I owe this point to H. Kogan and T. Packwood, *Advisory Committees and Councils in Education*, Routledge and Kegan Paul, 1974, p. 73.) 'The policy of positive discrimination', it said, 'is merely another expression of contemporary egalitarian dogma, the view that at every point the interest of those who have shown themselves capable of benefiting from education should be subordinated to those who show no wish to receive it.' If you concentrate your whole attention on making the race possible for the crippled, the swift and athletic will have no decent race to run. This is the thought. The fact is that neither Crosland nor the Plowden Report nor anything else can totally eliminate the notion that there is an educational ladder, a competition, a race. And such thinking must be, to a certain extent, realistic, as long as there are different jobs and roles in society, some of which demand, as others do not, a lengthy and academic education. As long as one thinks in competitive terms, the idea of equality of opportunity is bound to remain an ideal, however vaguely it is conceived. To try to eliminate this ideal, or to make people think that it is shameful to pursue it is no more satisfactory or rational or likely to benefit mankind than it would be to attempt to eliminate the notion of 'doing well for oneself' in general. To remove the concept of the ladder may well be to remove hope, and, it must be said, hope extends naturally to one's children's lives, perhaps even more than to one's own. Many people feel it is wrong or inappropriate to aim for too much for themselves, but these same people would feel purposeless and futile if they could not aim to 'better' their children. For the satisfaction of *this* desire, the ideal of equality of opportunity remains essential.

However, since there are theoretical difficulties with regard to determining what counts as equality of opportunity, and since much of what used to seem to ensure it, seems, if anything, now to ensure the opposite, and since we know neither what social engineering could accomplish nor how much of it we should be prepared to tolerate in the interests of equalizing opportunities, the notion of such equality cannot provide *by itself* a coherent theory on which to rest the distribution of education. There is another drawback as well. The notion of the educational ladder is applicable essentially to individuals who manage to start the climb. It depends, as we have seen, on the idea that there is a lower stage and a higher stage, with a few people making the ascent from one to the other. The general tendency, however, of social thought nowadays is to deal with groups or classes of people rather than with individuals. Marxist theory and sociology have had a general and widespread effect on our thought even if we are not Marxists or sociologists. It is no longer adequate to talk of the chances of individuals, largely, as we have seen, because an individual is thought to be what he is at least partly in virtue of being a member of the sociological group to which he belongs. So the idea of him as a separate unit who happens to have the characteristics he has, is a bit of mythology which is not only theoretically without interest, but also damaging, if pursued. For it may distract our attention from all the other people who are not he, but are members of the same group. The old-fashioned Samuel Smiles notion of self-help, of pulling one's solitary self up by the bootstraps is both irrelevant and immoral in social theory. The sources of this change in thinking may be in dispute, but its consequences are manifest (not the most agreeable of which is the tendency of right-wing theorists to claim to be the only defenders of the individual).

All the practical difficulties remain. The concept of the educational ladder, even if it is ineliminable from everyday thought about education, cannot provide any answers to the kinds of question which press upon policy makers. It cannot help to determine who shall be educated, for how long in what kinds of schools, or subject to what testing. To none of these problems does the idea of equality of opportunity have anything that is specific to contribute. One is tempted therefore as a theorist to return to the idea of equality not of opportunity, but of the actual stuff, education, which is to be distributed. We have already seen some of the difficulties involved in thinking of education in this light. Must equality in distribution of education therefore be given up—or treated as only at best, a vague and unreliable guide?

Rather than going back over these questions, let us try a fresh start: let us consider certain related principles, in case any of them is more powerful or illuminating than that of equality itself as a basis for educational distribution. These are the principle of envy, the principle of justice and the principle of compassion. I shall examine them in turn. First, envy. I am not, of course, suggesting that the principle of envy should be adopted as a standard in the distribution of education, but it is necessary to look at it, since, as is the case with the distribution of wealth, it is fairly closely similar to the principle of equality, to the extent that some people try to dismiss or devalue the idea of equality on the grounds that it is identical with envy and therefore, obviously, to be discouraged. There is an amusing formal account of envy in Chapter 8 of Nozick's book, *Anarchy, State and Utopia*. Briefly, as he says, 'The envious man prefers neither one having it [whatever "it" may be] to the other's having it and he not having it.' It should be clear from this definition how close is the connexion between envy and egalitarianism. For if equality were genuinely the highest or most important value, then it would be objectively better if neither of two people had some good than if one had it and the other did not. So one might think of egalitarianism as a kind of extension or generalization of envy. If I am thinking of myself and another person, it is envy; if I am thinking in general terms of any two people, whether or not one is myself, it is egalitarianism. (And this is why it is so irritating to be told that egalitarianism *is* envy: it suggests that one is incapable of impersonal argument; that all values really relate to oneself, and that 'good' always means 'good for me'.) But in fact this extreme egalitarianism is usually mitigated, as we have seen, by the more complicated idea of fairness, namely that goods should be distributed either according to desert or to need. So the unequal upshot can be explained and justified by the different needs or deserts of the parties to the distribution. We shall return to the question of need at the end of the chapter. As for merit, it is highly suspect. For not only is it very difficult to measure merit fairly, but, as we have seen, being someone with merit may not be a natural unchangeable 'internal' quality of a person but may be something which is itself subject to fair or unfair distribution. Perhaps it is worth trying to explain why envy arises, why, that is, we should mind someone else having something which we do not have, why we should mind it more than we mind our not having it and him not having it either. It cannot after all be entirely to do with the desire we feel for the good in question, otherwise the very central feature of envy, that we would prefer no one to have it rather than him to have it and not me, would not be present for, if I have not got it anyway, his having it should be no worse. There is a fairly obvious connexion between this feature of envy and self-esteem. Nozick makes this point well: he argues that how we esteem ourselves is always relative to how we esteem others. 'There is no standard of doing something well, independent of how it can be done by others. . . . It may injure one's self-esteem and make one feel less worthy as a person to know of someone else who has accomplished more or risen higher.' The more one's rival seems to merit his success, the more injurious it is to one's own self-esteem. If a violinist becomes world famous through great natural talent, or through natural talent and hard work combined, if I am a violinist, then I may think less of myself because of his meriting so much. And to think less of oneself is always disagreeable. Of course if I have no talent as a violinist at all, then I am not put out by his success because he is in no sense a rival; and if I have talent but am somehow prevented from using it by fate or chance (if I suffer an accident which permanently incapacitates my bowing arm, let us say) then I no longer feel any sense of injury at his being better. For a different reason I can again take myself out of the contest. But if I am an aspirant violinist, who somehow does not succeed as well as another, and if I cannot put this down to accident or fate, then I must think worse of myself than I would have if I had never heard of his success. The argument from self-esteem, the suggestion, that is, that this is what lies behind envy, is closely similar to the argument frequently deployed against any system of educational distribution which entails a 'ladder' of success. For it is often said that success on the ladder necessarily entails the notion of failure among those who do not succeed. To be dubbed a failure, so this argument runs, is harmful and intolerable, and therefore it is genuinely better that no one should succeed than that some should succeed and some should fail. This argument is not, it should be noticed, itself an argument from envy; it is only *like* an argument from envy. The crucial difference is that those who use it wish to remove the element of competition from education, to remove the whole notion of success and failure, not for their own sakes, but for the sake of the whole class of children involved. They are, as it were, being envious vicariously. For the sake of the failed children, they prefer that there should be no prize. But true envy cannot be vicarious. It is essentially a self-regarding emotion. I can be truly envious only if *I* am the person done down. Nevertheless the similarity between the two arguments is important. The egalitarian argument, though admittedly other-regarding, may not be rational. It may be irrational, first, in the sense of being impossible; for to remove the notion of the ladder would be to remove the notion that some education was higher than other education, and even if one could somehow suggest that no education was better than any other, still it seems that some would be higher, in the sense that it went on longer or came at a more advanced stage. Secondly the argument might be irrational in the sense that it would be destructive, if it were possible to do what was suggested, of something which in fact is an end very widely desired. But whether or not this is so depends on considerations other than those of equality. Other values are involved. So, once again, we seem to have reached the position where some different considerations have to be brought to bear on the arguments which concern themselves with equality.

Secondly we should consider the more respectable principle of justice or fairness itself. Justice (justice-as-fairness) has come in for a great deal of discussion in the last few years on account of the work of John Rawls, who in his monumental book *A Theory of Justice* (Oxford, 1972) has argued that these twin concepts form the centre of morality and are the only possible alternatives to a barren and unsatisfactory utilitarianism. Our question must be whether justice in Rawls's sense is a key to the distribution of education, and whether it is a concept able to overcome some or all of the difficulties and limitations which surround the idea of equality in this connexion. It is sometimes suggested (e.g. by Ian Lister in *New Society*, 15th May 1975) that the notion of equality is out of date since Rawls, and that it has been replaced, or should have been, by the notion of equity or fairness in distribution. Rawls himself, however, claims (*Op. cit.*, p. 100) that there is a sense in which his principles of distribution 'express an egalitarian concept of justice'. So, though equality is not, for him, a uniquely justifying concept, it nevertheless forms part of justice, and will be achieved if justice is achieved.

Rawls argues that the principles of fairness in distribution of any good are those that would be chosen by people in a co-operating society if they did not yet know and so could not yet take into account, their own special position in that society. He calls the hypothetical position from which they would choose 'the original position' and the choice they hypothetically make is made from behind a 'veil of ignorance'. I must confess to finding this whole notion extremely obscure. It is not clear how one would choose rationally (and the assumption is that it would be a rational choice, in fact this is insisted on) if one were as ignorant as Rawls sometimes suggests. For instance, one is supposed to be ignorant of one's own concept of the good. Nor is it clear who is supposed to constitute the choosing body. It is the people of one society, but is it everyone, or people of one period only, or people timelessly? However, it is perhaps unnecessary to enter into detail, or press this imaginative supposition too hard. Very broadly, the point of the original position and the veil of ignorance is to ensure that people in making a rational choice, should not be in a position to make exceptions in their own favour, or bias their decisions according to their own interests. This is the function of ignorance: they do not know where their own interests lie. It is a way of forcing us to consider a choice in its universal application. Would we want it to happen to us, whether we were at the giving or the receiving end? It is an elaborate device for making us adopt what Hume refers to as 'A steady and general point of view'; it is a version of the test of Kant's categorical imperative: Could we will that what we have chosen became a universal law?

Now in society people are unequal; some are better, some worse off. The just principle of distribution which they use in their rational choice from the original position (known as the principle of difference) is that the better off shall have more, only provided that in having more they benefit the worse off. There shall, that is to say, justly be an unequal distribution if and only if the worse off would have been *even* worse off had the distribution been equal. To a certain extent, equality is preserved; for the first principle of distribution is that basic rights and duties are equally distributed. But the second principle, which is our concern, is that social and economic inequalities are just only if they result in compensatory benefits for everyone and in particular for the least advantaged members of society. 'There is no injustice in the greater benefits earned by a few provided that the situation of persons not so endowed is thereby improved' (p. 15). The supposition is that you would choose this kind of distribution even if you did not know whether you were going to be better or worse off in real life.

The point of this second principle of distribution, the principle of difference, is to show that some real life inequalities may be just. Thus, to apply the argument to education, it may be just, according to Rawls's theory, that some people should have more education or better education than others if, by the existence of this disparity, it can be shown that the less well-educated actually benefit. For example, if it can be shown that the existence of a highly educated minority of surgeons ensures that the less educated non-surgeons benefit (as well as the surgeons themselves who not only get more education but presumably more money as well) then there is no injustice in this unequal distribution of education in favour of surgeons. This beneficial inequality is supposed to be obvious both to surgeons and to non-surgeons, and so it might be rationally chosen behind the veil of ignorance. Rawls's theory is in general an attempt to show that justice is rational, and incidentally that it is not the same as equality, although a just society would tend towards equality.

But its application to education seems very dubious, even if it has other merits. For the suggestion is that the sole criterion for the acceptability of educational differences should be the advantage of the less well educated. Now this is a justification in terms of service which certainly has a lot to be said for it; but it is fraught with difficulties. For one thing, it says nothing about the justice or otherwise of deciding *who* shall have the advantage of being educated (say to be a surgeon) and who shall not. Rawls sometimes speaks as though there were no difficulty at all in deciding this, as though those with talents just separated themselves out automatically. He speaks (p. 101) of 'those who have been favoured by nature', and of the 'distribution of natural talents' as though those who had them and those who had not were as readily distinguishable as are those who have and who have not got red hair. Then we have spoken of a natural talent for surgery. But there are also, presumably, natural talents which cannot be used to make the less well-endowed better off, or only very dubiously. If I have a natural talent for dancing is it obvious that my expensive education in dancing is justified by the fact that you, who have no talent and may not even like dancing anyway, can have the advantage, though your education was cheap, of going to see me dance? 'better off', 'the good of the less advantaged'. How are we to interpret these phrases? Are you better off for the chance to watch me dancing, even though if I had not been so well educated you might have learned to sew? (You might be so bad at sewing that you needed *special* education before you could even mend the rags you are wearing in your disadvantaged state.) Such problems are, obviously, the real and pressing problems when it comes to allocating resources to education in actual societies. But it seems to me that their solution is no more easily reached by an appeal to justice-as-fairness than it is by an appeal to equality. Neither principle is sufficient by itself. Once again, we need some further principle, or very likely more than one, to help us settle these questions of distribution.

Finally, we must look briefly at the principle of compassion or welfare. This is a far more difficult principle to document than that of justice or even of envy. It is seldom made explicit. Yet it is, as I suggested at the beginning of the chapter, very closely connected with the idea of equal distribution; and I would suggest that in fact it operates more generally as a motive for egalitarian reform than might always be allowed. For it is a principle which people are not always willing to avow. Although it is nice to seem concerned and to appear to care for men as one's brothers, there is also a stigma attached to paternalism; and compassion is akin to charity, often thought to be the virtue most studiously to be avoided. But was the motive force behind the positive discrimination arguments, for instance, really a passion for equality? I doubt it. It seems far more likely that it was mostly a sense of outrage and of pity that any children should have to live and grow up in such hopeless situations. To quote Crosland again (at the beginning of his chapter on equality of wealth in *The Conservative Enemy*): 'Inequality of living standards in Britain is greater than should be tolerated in a democracy. The contrasts between the lives of the better and worse off is offensive to compassion and humanity, let alone to socialist principles.' The implication here is that compassion and humanity are motives to be found in everyone, not only in socialists, and that therefore they are the most universal and inescapable motives to which to make appeal. It is surely true that even those who genuinely do not care much about equality will care for these, and that the desire for equality, where it does exist, may well be founded on nothing but a sense of 'compassion and humanity'. If we apply this principle, then, to the problems of distribution of education, we find ourselves back with R. H. Tawney (*Equality*, 1931): 'What a wise and good parent will desire for his own children, a nation must desire for all children.' There, quite explicitly, speaks the voice of paternalism. It was this voice which spoke through the reports of the Hadow Committee of the twenties (a committee of which Tawney was a member) and the Plowden Report on Primary Education of 1967. All children have educational as well as other needs, and it is these needs which the nation ought to satisfy, as a good parent will seek to satisfy them for his own family. But if education is distributed according to need then gross inequalities should automatically disappear, since at least in early childhood the needs of all children are the same. Of course what is accepted as educational need will change from time to time, according to the level of sophistication or civilization of society. While the battle was raging for secondary education for all it had to be argued that there could be a need for education which would continue for everyone beyond the age of thirteen. Now so much and more would be easily accepted. J. S. Mill thought that every parent had a duty to provide for his children not only food for their bodies but instruction and training for their minds, an education for each child that is 'fitting him to perform his part well in life towards others and towards himself' (*On Liberty*, Chapter V). Such an education, he suggested, would consist in giving to the child the ability to read and to acquire and retain a 'certain minimum of general knowledge'. Other people have later preferred as we have seen, to speak of educational needs not in terms of certain kinds of knowledge which children need to have, but of certain kinds of growth or flourishing in which they need to be encouraged. Obviously this latter kind of formula has of itself consequences with regard to the distribution of education. For there are some children who cannot learn to read and for whom the acquisition and retention of general knowledge must always remain practically an impossibility too. But such children can also be thought to grow and flourish, or to wither and suffer if they do not receive the kind of education which will enable them to develop the potential they have, however it compares with the potential of normal children. So at once the concept of needs in terms of the development of potential, lets in a whole group of children among whom education should be distributed, who, on a different view of need might have been thought simply ineducable. It is certainly not uninstructive to consider the education of the mentally handicapped in this connexion. For the doctrine of equality, even of positive discrimination in favour of the disadvantaged, has to be stretched to breaking point if it is to be used as the justification of educational effort and expenditure on the handicapped. But the doctrine of compassion can, obviously, justify it immediately, and without distortion. If we are humane, we will recognize a duty to improve the lot of all human beings, and particularly those who are most helpless.

So far, however, the attempts to define educational need which we have considered have been vague and general. The principle of compassion entails the notion of distribution according to need but it cannot any more than the principle of equality, actually determine the answers to the pressing practical questions. All it can do is show that one cannot answer the question 'to whom should education be given?' without also answering questions about what it is that should be given. We need to examine not the rule for handing the stuff out, but what the stuff should be. From now on, therefore, increasingly, we must turn our attention to matters of content, that is of the educational curriculum.

II

Equality as a Curriculum Aim

We have not finished with equality yet. For, though it is time to turn from considering the distribution of education to the question of what is to be taught, there are at least two respects in which the idea of equality inevitably reappears.

First, I have spoken, albeit with reservations, about education as though it were a commodity to be handed out to a passive, waiting consumer. But this image, that of the hungry sheep waiting to be fed, or of the patient queueing up for his medicine, although well worn, may not be a good one. It may reflect a false picture of education which will lead to bad practice. Are pupils mere receivers of goodies from on high? And if they are, should they be? Should teachers adopt a godlike role, or even the role of a pedlar with his wares? Should they not rather allow the pupils to lead in the very definition of the wares themselves? If the ideal of education as a kind of growth (rather than as the receiving of stuff to be consumed) is to be realized, then perhaps we ought to be looking in a rather different direction. For it might be that a condition of growth is self-determination. To be a mere receiver or consumer might be actually stunting. On this view, the teacher should not dictate things to his pupils. Although the pupil's role is to learn (this is what education consists in) the teacher's role need not necessarily be to teach, if this entails that he is active while his pupil is passive. Such a concept of education calls in question the authority of the teacher to determine what is to be taught. And in so doing it re-introduces the idea of equality. For the pupil and teacher are now represented as together engaged on equal terms in the process of pupil-growth. This picture, if accepted, would make a great difference not only to the manner and style of classroom life, but also to the matter, the actual content of the curriculum.

There is a second respect, closely connected with the first, in which it is necessary to consider equality again. If we are agreed that children have a right to be taught (an equal right to education) and if we can go further and think in terms of educating children according to their needs, then the question arises whether this is to be done by providing a common curriculum for everyone, or whether, as their needs are thought to be different, different children should be taught according to different curricula. The issue can be put quite crudely. Does equality in the distribution of education, or even equality of educational opportunity, mean everyone being 'introduced' to a common culture, or does it mean everyone participating in the culture in which he will in fact flourish, a culture which may, in some cases, be more familiar to him than to his teachers, who will have to learn from him as much as he from them? If this is what equality of distribution demands, there will be repercussions both on the relationship between teacher and pupil, and on the content of the curriculum in any given school.

So, although in the last chapter we considered equality in the context of distribution which is where it seemed to belong, and although I tried to distinguish questions of distribution from those of content, it turns out that this distinction cannot be so very clearly made. At any rate the notion of equality seems to spill over from the one area to the other. In the present chapter, I shall try to confine myself to this overlap. A more detailed consideration of curriculum content will be deferred until Chapter III.

Let us look first at the question of the authority of the teacher. How godlike are teachers to be? There is one simple point to be made here, which is curiously underplayed in much of the discussion of this topic, and that is that education is largely of children. Children gradually grow older, but when they are young, even if they are referred to as 'pupils' or 'students', they need grown-up persons to look after them, both for their safety and their happiness. Often, when reading discussions of how teaching should proceed or what is the proper method of education, one has no indication what stage of education is under consideration, what age-group is supposed to be at the receiving end, until suddenly a reference to a class of nine-year-olds, or some other specific age-group, brings one into touch with particular reality, and the whole of the previous discussion has to be reappraised. The fact is that when we discuss the authority of the teacher it will make a great difference, first, whether we are talking about school or university, and if school, whether primary or secondary. To confine our attention to schools, it will be necessary that at *all* stages of school life some authority is exercised by the teachers or some other adults. For, as long as children are at school, even when they are sixteen or seventeen, they are in the charge of the adults; they are to some extent the legal responsibility (for instance in case of accidents) of the adults. This is a point generally readily enough acknowledged by pupils at school when they demand equality with their teachers. They agree that, if things go wrong, it is not they but their teachers, and especially their head teacher, who bears the responsibility. It follows from this that in some sense the authority of teachers (or other adult persons) over pupils must be recognized, even if this authority is limited in various ways. The question, therefore, whether at school teachers should be recognized to have *any* authority is hardly worth discussion. It is manifest that they should, and if this entails non-equality between teacher and pupil, then egalitarianism must be modified or abandoned as a social ideal in this particular context. However much the pupils are consulted with regard to the organization of the school or the maintaining of discipline within it, they cannot be regarded as ultimately responsible; and whoever *is* ultimately responsible must be recognized as the possessor of authority. Such considerations as these will hardly apply at all to universities, or at any rate will not apply in the same way.

But there is a different, though connected, question which may more profitably be discussed, and which relates both to schools and to universities, and that is the extent of the teacher's authority when he is actually teaching, in the classroom or in the lecture or the tutorial. The traditional view of this matter is expressed by R. S. Peters (*Ethics and Education*, George Allen and Unwin, 1966, p. 256). The authority of teachers, he argues, should be rationally related to their understanding of matters to do with the curriculum and with children. The teacher, that is to say, should be regarded as an authority; and in this sense should be deferred to. 'The question is whether a teacher is . . . put *in* authority because to a certain extent he is regarded as *an* authority of a provisional sort on what a community values.' The teacher, regarded in this light, will be someone who has something which his pupils have not, namely a knowledge of that which the community values, and it is his duty to share this knowledge with them. They will be the receivers and therefore in this limited sense inferior to the teacher. His authority will reside in his superiority with respect to knowledge. 'A person', writes Peters, 'who is genuinely an authority about something invests it with an aura. His enthusiasm for his chosen activity or form of awareness and his mastery of its intricacies lures others to be initiated into its mysteries. . . . A sense of curiosity and wonderment must be conveyed about questions which give an activity its point, together with a passion for precision in accepting or rejecting answers to them.' There seem to be two quite different ingredients here. One is the intrinsic discipline of the subject matter itself. If the subject to be taught is, say, the principle parts of certain Greek verbs, then it is essential, in the nature of the case, that a certain formal framework shall be respected. The very notion of 'principle parts' suggests an accepted form of classification, sometimes, admittedly, somewhat arbitrary, as to what counts as one verb, or what parts of the verb are to be deemed to exist. The teacher may accept the framework unquestioningly or he may discuss it in a preliminary way. But if this is the subject matter then at some stage the pupils must, even if provisionally, accept the framework, and get on with the business of learning the verbs. There are many other kinds of subject matter which, in an analogous way, impose their own discipline on teacher and pupil alike. It is within such discipline that teachers should be regarded, according to Peters, as authoritative.

But of course a teacher can be an authority on such a discipline without having, or at any rate without displaying, any particular enthusiasm for it. And Peters seems to suggest that he will not be regarded in the way in which an authority ought to be regarded unless he does manifest enthusiasm of a kind which is catching. It is certainly true that if he has this catching enthusiasm then his pupils are less likely to question his right to teach them the subject than if he has not. And in an ideal world probably teachers always would be genuinely enthusiastic and lead their pupils willingly along the road to knowledge. But Peters himself admits that it does not always happen this way. 'Even the most inspiring stimulating and competent teachers', he writes (*Op. cit.*, p. 266), 'sometimes come across pupils who will not submit to the discipline of the learning situation.' On occasions such as these, he says, 'Authority on its own may be ineffective; it may have to be backed by power.' Now it seems to me that in saying this, Peters is admitting that, as we have seen, in the last resort teachers, even teachers in the classroom, have ultimate responsibility for imposing a form of discipline on their pupils such that the pupils can learn something. If they learn nothing, then there is cause to complain. So we are back at the point where there is a lack of equality between teacher and pupil, necessarily. In the ideal situation, where the teacher does inspire his pupils with enthusiasm for the subject, and they want to learn (or even in the very common situation in which they want to learn in order to pass an examination, whether they are enthusiastic or not) the lack of equality which is fundamental may be concealed, or may never be thought of at all. But teaching nevertheless entails such a lack.

Even in a university this is true. The only difference is that the question is seldom likely to arise in the actual lecture hall or seminar room. It is assumed, generally correctly, that for motives variously high or low the pupils wish to learn what the teacher has to teach. If they do not, they simply absent themselves from what is now generally called the 'teaching situation'. But if they are there and refuse to submit to 'the discipline of the subject' then as long as the teacher continues to attempt to teach them, he must thereby also attempt to exert a legitimate authority over them. He has rights, as long as he is teaching. Peters confuses the issue by confounding the demands of the subject matter with the enthusiasm of the teacher. But his non-egalitarian conclusion is right; right, that is to say, as long as we continue to think in terms of teaching and of specialization by subject disciplines in the traditional way.

And so the question of what the curriculum is actually to be, what subjects are to be taught, or whether what is to be taught should be thought of in terms of subjects at all raises itself inevitably here. I want to postpone the detailed discussion of it until the next chapter. But at this stage it is necessary at least to prepare for this discussion by introducing some of the criticisms which have been strongly made of the traditional (or Peters) point of view. There is no shortage of such criticism, sometimes violently expressed. First let us look at a comparatively neutral, sociological argument about the connexion between specialization and authority. In an article in *New Society* (14th September 1967) Basil Bernstein wrote as follows: 'Until recently the British educational system epitomized the concept of purity of categories' (what I have referred to as 'specialization'). 'The concept of knowledge was one that partook of the sacred; its organization and dissemination was intimately related to the principles of social control. . . . Specialization makes knowledge safe and protects the vital principles of social order. Preferably knowledge should be transmitted in a context where the teacher has maximum control or surveillance, as in hierarchical school relationships or the university tutorial relation. . . . Education in depth, the palpable expression of purity of categories, creates monolithic authority systems serving élitist functions.' Bernstein's point is that in a school or university in which there is specialization, each specialist teacher, an authority in his own subject, exercises authority over his pupils, and is also relatively autonomous in relation to the rest of the teaching staff. In the latter relation he may, it is true, be equal with his fellows, but in relation to his pupils, he will be superior in the hierarchy. He will be one of the authorities 'who . . . view their own know-ledge . . . with the jealous eye of a threatened priesthood'. The analogy with the priesthood is important here, for it paves the way inevitably to other, more violent, attacks on the hierarchical implications of the traditional view of the teacher/pupil relation. In a philosophically naïve and somewhat ill-mannered article by David Adelstein, for example (' "The Philosophy of Education" or the Wisdom and Wit of R. S. Peters' in *Counter Course*, edited by Trevor Pateman, Penguin, 1972), there is a discussion of the traditional view of the authority of the teacher. 'It is an illusion,' he writes, 'a masquerade of certainty and authority, a crass picture of mystification'. The entire view of education 'is a pretence that something significant is taking place'. And referring to Peters, he concludes, 'The problem of "educating people", a phrase which he uses frequently, reveals the essential élitism in his attitudes, and forgets that the educator must him-self be educated. It therefore divides the process into two parts: those who do the thing and those to whom it is done. This in-herent division gives rise to the teacher as authority and ulti-mately to the whole class division of society which is mediated in the educational system.' In an earlier book, in much the same style, we find the following among the 'messages' supposed to be carried by the traditional medium of teaching (*Teaching as Subversive Activity*, Neil Postman and Charles Weingartner, Penguin, 1971, pp. 31 and 50): That passive acceptance is a more desirable response to ideas than active criticism; that discovering knowledge is beyond the power of students and is in any case none of their business; that the voice of authority is to be trusted and valued more than independent judgement; that there is always a single unambiguous right answer to a question. The very features of the teacher's authority emphasized by Peters, his enthusiasm and conscious expertise, are listed as dis-barring him from taking part in genuine education. 'There are thousands of teachers who teach "subjects" such as Shakespeare, or the Industrial Revolution, or geometry because *they* are inclined to enjoy talking about such matters. In fact that is why they became teachers. It is also why their pupils fail to become competent learners.' Here the basis of the attack is not that teachers wrongly regard themselves as experts, or authorities, but rather that they wrongly regard teaching as a matter of handing on an expertise. Teaching is not, so the argument goes, a sharing of knowledge which the teachers have and their pupils do not. Rather the teacher and the taught should be regarded as co-operating on a footing of equality in the solving of certain problems.

Equality between the participants is essential to a thorough-going 'enquiry' theory of education. An 'enquiry teacher', we are told (*Op. cit.*, p. 43), 'rarely tells the student what he thinks they ought to know. . . . His lessons develop from the responses of students and not from a previously determined "logical" structure. Almost all of his questions . . . are aimed at having his students clarify a problem, make observations relevant to the solution of the problem, and make generalizations based on their observations. His goal is to engage students in those activities which produce knowledge.' Finally the authors suggest that the very notion of teaching is misleading in this sort of context, because of the authoritarian, hierarchical implications contained in it. 'Perhaps there is need to invent a new term or name for the adult who is responsible for arranging the school learning environment.'

It is not merely in terms of method that enquiry or discovery forms of education are more egalitarian than traditional forms. It is not, that is to say, simply that if the means of instruction is less a matter of making statements and more a matter of asking questions, the teacher will necessarily be less obviously 'set above' the pupil. There are at least two further suggestions. First, there is the suggestion that pupils are in some way just as likely to 'produce knowledge' by their activities as teachers are; all that the teacher has, which the pupil has not, is the resources, and perhaps the adult competence, to set up a kind of environment in which knowledge may be generated. If there is an existing body of knowledge with which he is acquainted and his pupils are not, then as far as possible he should conceal this. And if he is interested in it and enthusiastic (likes talking about it) he has no business to indulge himself. Secondly, there is perhaps the hint of a further reason for equalizing pupil and teacher, a reason expressed with characteristic imprecision by Dewey. Education, according to Dewey, must be through experience, and the discipline inherent in educational as opposed to non-educational or random experience is the discipline imposed by a student adapting his enterprise to the enterprise of others involved in the same general purpose. Learning, that is to say, involves the constraint of working with someone else to a common end. In this way all learning should be *democratic*. 'A democracy is more than a form of government; it is primarily a mode of associated living, of conjoint communicated experience.' (Quoted by Sidney Hook, *Op. cit.*, p. 27.) All good education should be an exercise in this kind of associated living; and so the pattern of the classroom should be a pattern of co-operation and common understanding of an end or an interest. It is not wholly clear what this amounts to; but at any rate it seems to lead away from the teacher as embodying authority, and towards the concept of free enterprise among equals.

Now there are various (probably well worn) objections to the enquiry method of education. But in the first place we may consider a relatively pedantic point. If enquiry is correlated with 'discovery' then a good deal of education must be enquiry-based, for there is a sense in which a great deal of it must be a matter of discovery, namely all of that very important part of education which consists in learning skills. In the discussion of the relation between teacher and pupil which we have looked at so far, very little is explicitly said about the teaching of skills. But at least if we are thinking in terms of school teaching, a vast proportion of what goes on at school should be so described. Reading and writing, understanding and speaking a foreign language, using various machines, calculating, playing musical instruments: all of these are skills. And if my teacher is teaching me to play the horn, then it is unlikely that he will simply enunciate propositions. He will show me, help me to practise, give me tips (along with some theory, no doubt) and the hoped-for result will be that I shall discover how to play. The discovery of techniques is discovery, and if it makes anyone feel happier, the subject matter of my horn lesson can be posed in terms of a question, 'How can I sustain this long note without altering pitch?' or some other such problem. In this kind of case there is no conflict whatever between the perception of the teacher as expert and the aim of the lesson being that the pupil should discover something. This constitutes not so much an objection to the enquiry method as a willing acceptance of it.

However, a genuine objection to enquiry methods is that they may well entail a good deal of fake and pretence. Adelstein's picture of the traditional teacher was of a man pretending to expertise, to a superiority he did not really have. But as much, or more, pretence is involved if a teacher has to pretend that he is not providing his pupils with answers, or at least dictating their questions, when he really is. The model of Socrates, often employed for the non-hierarchical teacher, is, after all, a somewhat unfortunate one. For nothing could possibly be more artificial, not to say bogus, than the famous passage in the *Meno* where Socrates is portrayed as leading the slave to display his knowledge of geometry. And many of the modern versions of eliciting answers to questions may be equally ritualistic. Speaking for instance of the 'good' non-authoritarian teacher, Postman and Weingartner say: 'The only kind of lesson plan or syllabus that makes sense to him is one that tries to predict . . . and deal with the authentic responses of learners to a particular problem, the kinds of questions they will ask, the obstacles they will face, their attitudes, the possible solutions they will offer.' (*Op. cit.*, p. 45.) But it might be argued that this kind of lesson-plan may be just as restrictive and tyrannical as the old kind. If the teacher is obliged to predict responses, will he be able to deal with the unpredictable response? If he has to foresee obstacles, will he not feel obliged to mention these obstacles and difficulties, even if his pupils have not noticed them? The difference between this and 'ordinary' teaching becomes very obscure: the only addition seems to be that the enquiry teacher, like a skilful negotiator, has to pretend that the other party had the ideas himself.

Now the authors are perfectly aware that there is likely to be something unrealistic and absurd about pupils attempting 'discovery' or 'free enquiry' about subject matter, suggested to them by a conscientious 'enquiry method' teacher, but about which they have no actual desire to learn. 'It is sterile and ridiculous', they write (p. 59), 'to attempt to release the enquiry powers of students by initiating studies that hold no interest for them. Have you ever seen such a performance? For instance the use of the enquiry method to discover the characteristics of pendulums or the forms of verbs? It is a kind of intellectual minuet—all form and no substance.' The suggestion, then, becomes the more radical one, that it is only if the actual subject matter of the enquiry is changed, so that the pupils are interested in it, that the element of pretence will be eliminated. It is worthy of note, in passing, that the enquiry lessons quoted with approval by these authors almost all turn out to be on questions such as 'what counts as a rule?' 'Is there one and only one sense of "right" and "wrong"?' 'can there be different versions of the truth?' 'what counts as a fact or as truth?' and so on. All these questions are, roughly speaking, philosophical. And there is no doubt at all that children of all ages, as well as grown-ups, enjoy talking about them. But even the most extreme proponent of the co-operative or enquiry method of education, or the most self-interested professional philosopher, would hardly suggest that this is to be the whole content of the school, or indeed the university, curriculum. And even when philosophy is the subject, a teacher will probably be better as a philosopher than his pupils and will certainly have more expertise. We will postpone further discussion of what else besides philosophy ought to be included, for the time being.

There is another point to be made, however, before leaving the dangers of pretence in enquiry teaching. Even supposing that a subject has been found in which the pupils are genuinely interested, and supposing that they are sufficiently mature to initiate some enquiries, discover evidence and make generalizations from this evidence, there is still, it seems to me, a danger that they may believe themselves to have made some contribution to knowledge when they have not. There tends to be a confusion in the discussion between what is a contribution to knowledge and understanding in general, and what is a contribution to a pupil's own knowledge. That there should be such a confusion is of course not surprising, since the whole notion of a body of knowledge in which one may become expert is itself under fire. I shall return to this point as well in the next chapter. But there is a temptation to suggest to pupils that their kind of research is real research; that they have, by enquiring, entitled themselves to make broad conclusions, when in fact, in the nature of the case, they can have looked at only a minute section of the relevant evidence.

Worse still, it is extremely common to find pupils whose enquiry takes them to an encyclopedia or textbook, or whatever book happens to be available on the school library shelf. And because they have gone to the trouble to look something up, even perhaps to go as far as the public library to do so, they are inclined to suppose that this gives their answer a kind of authority which it would not have if they had simply been told it by their teacher. They accept the authority of the author of the article in the encyclopedia as god-given, though they are taught not to accept that of their teacher. I do not want to belittle the worth of training children to look things up in books, or of training them to ask questions, of all kinds of people other than their teachers. But it is dangerous to lead them to believe that what they get by these methods is somehow final. It is, after all, much easier to make allowances for the quirks and prejudices of one's teacher whom one knows, and so take what he says with a pinch of salt, than it is to make similar allowances for the author of a textbook or article, whom one does not know. Sometimes the enquiry method can lead to a greater dogmatism than the alleged dogmatism of the more traditional method.

Another kind of objection to the enquiry or co-operative version of learning is perhaps most closely related to the view of learning as democratic; and since this view, as we have seen, was only vaguely and ambiguously formulated by Dewey, so the objection to it must itself remain somewhat vague. But in so far as education is thought of in this light, it certainly seems to

68

tend towards a new kind of orthodoxy, the orthodoxy of 'togetherness' or '*Mitsein*'. Why should one always be supposed to learn more, or to learn more worthwhile things, by working with other people than by oneself? For the essential element in the theory that the teacher and pupil should be equal partners in an educational adventure of some kind is that they should work *together*: all the pupils and their teacher are working together towards finding things out, wherever the argument leads them. But one crucial way of learning is to allow one's own imagination to escape, to find significance in things where it can, alone. We shall return to this point in Chapter IV. What is abusively referred to as the alienation of the pupil from the traditional syllabus may be the necessary foundation of his being able to use it as his own possession, his own starting point for the exercise of his intelligence in his own way (and only so, incidentally, can he ever come to interest himself in things which at first he thought would be boring). Consider Dewey again (*Democracy and Education*, New York, Macmillan, 1966, p. 143): 'The idea of perfecting an "inner" personality is a sure sign of social divisions. What is called "inner" is simply that which does not connect with others . . . which is not capable of free and full communication. What is termed "spiritual culture" has usually been futile, with something rotten about it, just because it has been conceived as a thing which a man might have internally, and therefore exclusively.' But educationalists should not forget that, as J. S. Mill well knew, there is such a thing as the tyranny of the majority, and to succumb to that is just as much a death to the individual as is succumbing to the tyranny of *one* other person. Moreover, they should remember the paradoxical truth that the individual and his central imagination may well be able to flourish best against a background of routine, of discipline and of a certain degree of external restraint. Whether this is true of adults is not perhaps obvious, though I personally believe it. But it is certainly true of children.

Finally, it may be objected to enquiry methods that they tend, in so far as they are based on the current interests of the pupils, to give rise to a total relativism with regard to what is worth teaching. Anything will do as a subject of enquiry, provided only that the pupils are enthusiastic about it. Obviously in practice things are not usually as open as this; but in theory there seems no reason why they should not be so. Once again we are led back to the crucial question of the content of the curriculum. Can this be decided by reference only to the preferred method of teaching—by reference to the insistence that pupils and teacher should be equals, as seekers after knowledge, and as equally interested in what they are doing?

There are various further points to be considered before we can address ourselves to that question. First, we have so far dealt almost entirely with the relationship between pupil and teacher, and the teacher's authority at school. We should briefly look at the position with regard to students in universities or other places of higher education, though this is not our main or direct concern. It will be clear at once that not all the same considerations apply. The case for equality between teacher and student must surely be stronger. Both teacher and pupil in such a context are, after all, technically adult. Nevertheless it seems to me that many of the same questions arise here. If we are going to preserve any part of the traditional view of what is to be taught and learned at a university, then the *teacher as expert* will necessarily remain a key figure in the transaction. Indeed his importance will be, if anything, greater. For part of the purpose of school is, perhaps, to teach children to adopt certain attitudes to work and learning, and in some cases it may be thought that this can best be done by specifically getting them, albeit artificially, to practise certain techniques, of research, investigation and so on, no matter what the subject matter. But such general educational goals are no longer appropriate at university level, or at any rate should be subordinate to the more specific syllabus which the student has come to the university to pursue. He is, after all, there by choice, and he can be supposed to have decided that learning is what he wants. Therefore he must be considered to have voluntarily submitted himself to a discipline of learning and this entails the acceptance of authorities or experts in some fields.

At the same time, the element of mutal dependence between teacher and student for the advancement of learning is far greater than it was at school. Because university students have already learned, or are fast learning, the basic tools of their chosen subjects, the likelihood of their actually advancing its frontiers, seeing it in a creatively new light and illuminating it for its practitioners is appreciable. Moreover, the presence in a university of people actively engaged in research, many of whom will be the very same people who teach, has an immense effect on the attitude of students to their branch of study. Indeed it is crucial to this attitude that those teaching should not be thought of *primarily* as teachers but as persons engaged in academic work of a wider kind, not all of it connected with education. If this is understood then the threat of the teacher dogmatically dictating to his students what they must uncritically accept is much diminished (though of course the dangers so alarming to Postman and Weingartner that teachers will talk about what they are interested in will proportionately increase).

There is, however, a growing body of attack on universities and schools for the inequality between teacher and pupil, which is more radical and more overtly political than any so far considered. The main burden of the attack is, once again, that teachers exercise an unjustified domination over their pupils by pretending to an authority they have not got with regard to what is to be taught. As one might expect, this pretended authority is sometimes said to express itself in a particular kind of teaching, lecturing for example to a passive audience, rather than engaging in genuine discussion; but the criticism is more fundamentally directed towards content than towards teaching method.

Briefly, the argument is that no one has more right than anyone else to determine what should be taught. There is at this point an ambiguity which must be noticed but which perhaps cannot be wholly eliminated. For 'determining what should be taught' sometimes means determining what subjects should be taught, sometimes determining, within a given subject matter, what is to be accepted as true and what false or problematic. We can perhaps characterize these two interpretations as the more and the less moderate. According to the moderate interpretation, students may demand an equal right with their teachers to construct the course, or control the curriculum which is to be followed. This is generally demanded in an attempt to achieve relevance, but relevance takes on a rather different sense according to whether school or university is under discussion. At school, as we have seen, it is alleged that children cannot learn unless what they are learning is relevant or immediately interesting to them. At university, on the other hand, the demand is not based on the proposition that only relevant subjects can be learned, but rather that only they are *worth* learning. Whereas at school what was relevant was whatever could be supposed naturally to interest a child, at university what is relevant is taken to be whatever gives greater understanding of and control over the world of the present day. So sometimes the moderate claim for equality in the determining of courses is simply the demand that they should be brought up to date. Students determine the content of courses by having powers to extend them, for example, to cover more of contemporary literature, or less of the history of philosophy and more of what is going on, perhaps in remote parts of the world, but at the present time. This kind of demand can be sensible or silly, put forward politely or aggressively, but it is essentially moderate in that it is a matter of reform of an existing structure.

But alongside this kind of demand, there may go another more extreme attack not on the particular limitations of a given course, but on the general nature of the curriculum, any curriculum, as based on the teaching of supposed objective truth. This is the radical or Marxist attack on the authority of the teacher. A clear statement of it is to be found in an article by Rose Dugdale, published in 1972 (in *Counter Course*, edited by Trevor Pateman, Penguin, p. 159). She argues here that the reformist tradition which seeks to improve society by improving the ideas people are taught is nothing but hypocrisy. 'The nature of this hypocrisy is explained', she writes, 'by a quite distinct view of the relation between education, ideas, theory and society. . . . No longer are the ultimate causes of social change to be sought in the undetermined neutral progression of ideas, from the false into insight into eternal truth and justice. Ideas are themselves dependent upon, and developed for and within, a particular society ruled by a particular class.' There is no such thing, therefore, as a neutral theory or a neutral fact. The essential purpose of the student demand for equality with their teachers is to expose the pretence of neutrality which the teacher may assume. In another essay in the same volume, this time on history, Robbie Gray urges that specialization, the accumulation of knowledge, should be tolerated only in so far as it is absolutely essential for answering the questions which 'we' (presumably the students) want to raise about the past. Otherwise, whatever its particular subject matter, it is to be condemned. 'Specialization tends to deform history into a static body of knowledge. Some people have this knowledge, others must passively receive instruction. To teach instead that our historical consciousness rests on a problematic relationship between the past, ourselves as products of the past, and the concepts we use to give meaning to the past is immediately to diminish the authority claimed by the "professional historian".' (*Op. cit.*, p. 289.) He goes on: 'In the teaching situation superior knowledge is taken as conferring the right unilaterally to define the questions asked and the kind of evidence deemed relevant, thus preventing the development of a shared understanding.' And he concludes, 'Syllabus reforms will not basically alter this situation.' (It is perhaps worth noting in passing how the new teaching of history, like the new school teaching in general, turns out to be a kind of philosophy, concerned with the most abstract questions about the concepts we use.) Quotations could be multiplied. Steven Rose, for example, a professor in the Open University writes as follows: 'Scientists must understand and struggle against the undemocratic nature of science as an institution (its hierarchy . . . all power to the professors; its élitism . . . all power to the experts; its sexism . . . all power to the men; and its racism . . . all power to Western modes of thought).' He was quoted in an article by Paul Johnson (*The*

Times Higher Education Supplement, 31st October 1975), who also quotes the words of a student from the University of Kent: 'There is no one truth in which the university can educate us. We have to find our own version of the truth for ourselves, and what may be true for one person may well be untrue for another.' And in the course of the debate set in motion by the Paul Johnson article from which I quoted above, Martin Jaques from the University of Bristol wrote as follows (*TTHES*, 21st November 1975): 'Surely we are not still arguing about whether or not neo-classical economics, Namierian history, Leavisite criticism and Parsonian sociology contain ideological implications. Clearly they do.' The consequence he derives from this is predictable. Students have as much right as their teachers to 'govern' the university (and this presumably means that they should determine the syllabus to be taught). He says: 'Johnson's view ultimately seems to rest on an extremely hierarchical concept of knowledge. Thus the teaching process is, in effect, reduced to those who possess the knowledge, the academics, the active agents, transmitting it to those who don't, the students, the passive agents (sic).' The argument is that if all theories are ideology-laden, then any suggestion that those who 'know' are in a way superior to those who do not (the hierarchy of knowledge) must be false. And therefore the student and the teacher are with respect to knowledge in the same boat.

We must return to this and other questions as to the possibility of non-relative knowledge in the next chapter. In many ways the discussion of this question will prove to be absolutely central to the study of the problem of politics in education. Moreover, more than any other question raised in these pages, it is one upon which individual readers must have clear and coherent views.

So far we have seen that the most radical attack on the authority of the teacher is not that he dictates without right the content of the curriculum, that he chooses what subjects shall be taught, but rather that he illegitimately dictates *what is to count as true* and what false. Teachers pretend to the possession of a neutral or absolute standard of truth. In fact, according to this extreme view, there is no such standard. But in the general flux, the student has as much right to 'his' truth as the teachers have to 'theirs'. This anti-authoritarian argument is thus a plea for the irrational. None has more right to be heard than another, and if one party uses reason to 'prove' his version of the truth, this reason is only one among a variety of possible weapons (the one preferred by the bourgeois academic) and no more absolutely to be preferred than any other.

Egalitarianism on this scale becomes a totally new phenomenon, and the whole notion of teaching or being taught ceases to make any sense in its context. Moreover the universities themselves would surely wither away if the distinction between the true and the false were genuinely totally relative. And if the universities disappeared then ultimately schools, as we know them, would disappear too. But in fact universities will continue to exist just as schools will, as the settings in which knowledge increases, and progress in understanding, both for the individual and for society at large is achieved, for this is what people on the whole want of their schools.

So we must conclude that within school or university equality between teacher and pupil in this extreme sense cannot exist. In so far as the teacher must be an authority and must be treated as such, equality must be sacrificed; that is to say it must be abandoned in the classroom. To say this is not, however, to say that the teacher is the sole repository of truth, or that in order to teach he must believe himself to be in possession of the whole truth on any subject. To suggest this would be absurd, as any teacher would agree. Obviously in university and to a certain extent at school the teacher will be open to learning from all sources, including from his pupils, and as his pupils become more specialist, or more fully engaged in their own genuine research, so he will expect to learn more from them. But the fact remains that a teacher has been appointed partly in virtue of his knowledge, and to say this is to say that there is a standard of knowledge and of truth which it is his business to convey to his pupil. It is in the light of this fact that he is to be regarded as unequal.

The rejection of the extreme view of equality still leaves open the question who actually plans the curriculum, and according to what principles. In the case of university courses the answer seems to me relatively unproblematic. We must distinguish between deciding in general what courses there are to be, and actually planning the curriculum within a course. On the former question a number of considerations, many of them financial, will have to be brought to bear. But when this has been agreed, then broadly speaking those who settle on the content of the course are the academic professionals, into whatever bodies within the institution they may organize themselves. It is within the sphere of setting up the curriculum that the teachers above all have to rely upon their authority and expertise in their own subject. Students may advise, may express their wishes, may criticize, but it is essentially the business of the academics, the professionals, to establish both the overall curriculum and the details of the syllabus. As long as we are prepared to allow that there are experts, then that this is part of their job seems to me self-evident. One of the great merits of this system is that it will result in a variety of different courses. For different academics and experts will have different views, not so much on what is or is not true, as on what is important, or interesting or likely to be a fruitful preliminary to further advances in knowledge, and they will plan their curricula accordingly. And since, with regard to universities at least, these curricula are advertised, potential students can make informed choices before embarking on a particular course. At present, at any rate, they have freedom to choose what course to study, within the limitations imposed by the numbers of available places at the university.

But the whole thing is different at school. Even those few parents who can freely choose what school they will send their children to may still have virtually no choice of curriculum or course. There seems to be a kind of inevitability about what is to be learned at school. This is not necessarily a bad thing; but it does mean that at some time or other people must ask by what criteria school curricula are determined, and who is ultimately responsible for this kind of planning. Is there a way of settling what, in general, *ought* to be in the school curriculum? These are questions of the utmost importance, and everyone, in the long run, is affected by the answers to them. But so far are the questions from having clear answers that it is not even certain what *kind* of criteria are being considered. Are there, for example, some purely educational or pedagogic arguments in favour of one sort of curriculum rather than another? Or, on the other hand, must all such arguments be ultimately moral or political in nature? Or could it be perhaps all a matter of taste? In due course we must consider these possibilities.

But first there is one more question which arises directly and urgently out of the consideration of equality and which was referred to at the beginning of this chapter. Granted that equality of educational opportunity is an agreed goal, however difficult and confused the concept may be, then we face the question whether this goal demands that all children shall be taught according to the same curriculum, or whether the curriculum should be adapted to the child. An attempt to answer this question will occupy the remainder of this chapter.

It is obviously difficult to separate completely those arguments about curriculum which are based on considerations of equal opportunity from those which are based on other, perhaps more 'educational' grounds. Any attempt to do so involves a certain amount of artificiality, and it must not be forgotten in the account which is to follow, that those persons whose views are considered have very probably got other arguments, as well as those derived from equality, to support their conclusions. I would not be understood to be commenting on the whole of their cases at this stage but only raising the question whether one can make *any* progress in curriculum-planning by invoking equality as the criterion by which to distinguish good from bad curricula.

There seems at the present time to be two directions in curriculum-planning towards which the arguments from equality lead. The first is towards different curricula for different kinds of child. That there should be diverse curricula may seem at first sight a surprising conclusion to be drawn from the argument for equality. For it might seem obvious that if children are to have the *same* educational opportunities, they should all study the same subjects which should lead them, if they are able, to the same universities and to the possibility of the same employment. If some school education is suitable for potential doctors, let us say, then, it might be thought, all children must have this education if they are to have, all of them, an equal chance to become doctors if they wish to. And indeed it was the diversity of curricula, one curriculum for grammar school, one for technical school and one for secondary modern school, which finally seemed the gross injustice, the supreme unequalizer, of the 1944 Act. The argument against the Act was that it entailed discriminating among children at eleven, and selecting one sort of curriculum for one lot and another for another lot. It now seemed better, on the grounds of equality, to have every child in the same school, pursuing the same curriculum. But this anti-selection argument can be shown to rest ultimately on the 'ladder' view of educational opportunity—the view, that is to say, that education is competitive, that some will win, get to the top, others will lose. We have already seen objections to this view, ineliminable as I believe it to be. After all, for those who are too much disadvantaged to stand any chance at all in the competition, that there are excellent rules for competing may be small consolation. What they get in the end will certainly not be equality. The prizes are beyond them. Not only may they not be able to win, they may not even be able to *try* to win.

Following this line of argument, then, one reaches the proposition that a system in which some are *doomed* to failure while others can succeed cannot possibly be defended on grounds of equality, since the mere empty right to compete, though all may have the right, does not count as equality. What is needed is an equal chance to succeed, not just to compete. So if grossly disadvantaged children are to have this equality, it must be arranged that they can succeed in something else. And so the position is reached in which it is argued that what a child is taught must depend upon what he is, and in what he is capable of succeeding. Both his environment and his capabilities of understanding must

78

be taken into account in establishing a curriculum for him. For environmental factors will partly determine how far he can, to revert to the Dewey and Plowden metaphor, 'grow'.

It has been, of course, in the Plowden 'priority areas' that this kind of theory has seemed to have most obvious application. At first 'positive discrimination' was intended to make schools in priority areas as good as schools elsewhere; and the assumption was that with greater resources they would become *like* other schools, and teach much the same things. But gradually it began to look as if this would not do; for failure would still be the inevitable outcome for children who attended these schools. The alternative has been most energetically canvassed by Eric Midwinter (in, for instance, *Projections . . . an educational priority area at work*, Ward Lock, 1972). 'As it stands', he wrote, 'the educational system offers the same product to all. In trite terms, this is a ladder for all to climb. But as only a few can reach the top, it is in part an education for frustration. The rules of the game are indubitably the same for everyone: it's just that some of the participants are nobbled.' Earlier, in *The Times Educational Supplement* (January 1971), he had written: 'Different social groups require different types of school, and the idea of handing out dollops of compensation is false.' Those few out of the most disadvantaged class who do reach the top, or near it, leave the area where they were brought up. The rest remain with no understanding, he claims, of their own problems, or how these could conceivably be solved. This is because their education has been totally alien. It has been directed not towards goals they cannot reach, but towards the *sort* of goals they cannot even recognize as goals, so completely out of place are they in the depressed areas where the education was handed out. The opposite of such a remote and alien education is an education which, in Midwinter's words is *relevant* and *realistic*.

It should be noticed that the solutions proposed by Midwinter are genuinely radical. Obviously, as we have seen, there had long been somewhat diverse curricula in different types of secondary school; and the inequalities of life-chances to which this led had been heavily under fire. In the *Harvard Educational*

Review (1968), James Coleman distinguished various stages in the development of the concept of equal educational opportunity in a way that is relevant to the radical view. The first stage is the familiar ladder-concept, which entails that all children must be exposed to the same curriculum. 'The underlying idea was that opportunity resided in exposure to a curriculum; the community's responsibility was to provide the curriculum, the child's to take advantage of it.' But gradually the concept changed, as attention began to focus on the effects of school on different children, the results which came out of the school, rather than the resources and the teaching that went into it. 'The implication of the most recent concept', he wrote, 'is that the responsibility to create achievement lies with the educational institution, not with the child.' It is the duty of the school to propose goals which can be achieved. The end which the curriculum has in view, if it is to be realistic, must be an end which can be realized in the school itself. And the most radical suggestion of all is that the goal should be not success in the future but enjoyment in the present, an enjoyment which contains continuous success as an ingredient.

Alongside and overlapping this concept is that of the genuine community school. Instead of attempting to compensate for the inadequacies of the home, the school should simply attempt to establish a smooth relation with the home. 'The lesson of the successful middle-class school is that it identifies with its *environs*; this could point the road for many an Educational Priority Area school.' (Midwinter, *Projections*, p. 37.) The practical consequence of this, as far as the curriculum goes, is that it should be geared above all to 'the familiarization of the child with his immediate environment, in all its moods and manners, warts and all'. The great disadvantage to be avoided is 'schizophrenia'. Teachers are represented as themselves torn between two cultures; since some of them 'must figuratively as well as literally, praise Wordsworth by day and watch *Coronation Street* by night' (*Op. cit.*, p. 101). 'It is not a question', he says, 'of whether society's standards are worse or better than the schools' values; the question is, should they be different, with the constant threat of children being schizophrenically faced with dual standards?' If dual standards are to be rejected, what counts as an acceptable curriculum? The main criterion, on the Midwinter view, is, as we have seen, relevance. What is relevant may be included in the curriculum, what is irrelevant must go. And relevance is closely akin to familiarity. Thus a child in a city school will be given material which is urban and local. He will be posed questions which relate to the immediate city environment and it will be to these that he is to discover answers. Similarly, the country child will be offered rural topics. The overall aim being 'immediate enjoyment coupled with the exploration of relevant material'; there will in the end be as many different curricula as there are environments to which they are each relevant. 'One is thinking . . . not of two types but of many types of school. Schools should vary substantially according to the specific needs and nature of the communities they serve . . . each rural school could be dissimilar from the next, each downtown school unlike its neighbour, and so on.' (*Op. cit.*, p. 13.) Obviously, as things are, there already exist these dissimilarities. They arise inevitably out of the locality, the catchment area of the school, as well as out of the character of the head, and the personality and skills of the staff. But where the differences are too gross, what we may call normal egalitarian theory tends to frown. The Midwinter radical egalitarianism, on the other hand, smiles. For in each school the end would be to make 'the known, the taken for granted, more knowable' (*Op. cit.*, p. 11). Now in the very long run even the Midwinter philosophy looks beyond the present satisfaction of the pupils to some further, future end. For he speaks with feeling of the 'negative revolt of the smashed telephone kiosk' being replaced by 'the positive revolution of communities restoring themselves in accordance with their own concepts'. And of the relevant and realistic curriculum at school 'from which foundation the community might begin to revise its structure'. So it is possible that when the millennium comes and the classless society is a reality, then there will be one kind of school again with one kind of curriculum. But for the moment, that concept is to be rejected.

Midwinter is not alone in suggesting a multiplicity of curricula. G. H. Bantock, for example, has argued in many places that there should be an alternative, non-literary curriculum for the mass of the people, on the grounds that the masses of the working class have a tradition which is totally unsuited to literary studies, studies which are bound to remain alien and remote as far as they are concerned. (See, for instance, G. H. Bantock, 'Equality and Education', in *Education, Equality and Society*, edited by Bryan Wilson, George Allen and Unwin, 1975.) They need a practical, concrete curriculum, without too much reading. Such suggestions as these, however, seem to arise from a kind of despair at the actual failure of current educational practice, rather than from any very serious theoretical considerations. The interesting feature of Midwinter's proposals is that they arise from an egalitarian position; and the arguments against such a multiplicity of curricula, which seem to me to be absolutely conclusive, may also be derived from egalitarianism. For Midwinter himself acknowledges that there is force in the objection that his priority schools 'help create a ghetto or some kind of proletarian enclave'. His only answer to this is that he does not propose only two kinds of schools, but many. But of course to say this is not to prove that among the many the middle-class kind would not still seem superior. Many kinds of oppressed minorities can exist alongside each other without being therefore less despised, or even less oppressed. To have 'different' schools with socially orientated syllabuses may well simply entrench the position of the 'middle-class' syllabus offered in the smart school. Michael Young ('Curricula as Socially Organised Knowledge' in *Knowledge and Control*, Collier-Macmillan, 1971) makes the same point in relation to the Schools Council innovatory syllabuses designed for the less able. What he says could well be applied, not to particular syllabuses, but to 'special' curricula as a whole. 'These courses,' he writes, 'which explicitly deny pupils access to the kinds of knowledge which are associated with rewards, prestige and power in our society are given a kind of legitimacy which masks the fact that educational "success" in terms of them would still be defined as "failure".' This is a crucial point. If only those at the top of the ladder can get the kinds of jobs which bring prestige and power, it is of no use to pupils at school to make it totally impossible, not merely very difficult, for them to set foot on the ladder. However much they may grow up happy, having enjoyed school rather than hating it; however much they may now understand their own community, having studied it rather than the history of the Italian Renaissance, still the fact will remain that few of them, if any, will earn as much money or wield as much power as their neighbours up the hill, who also studied their culture and community, but whose culture happened to be concerned with national rather than local politics, with international languages rather than neighbourhood patois, and with the shared literature of the West rather than with the back of the *Radio Times*. Parity of esteem, as we all learned after the 1944 Act, does not come of itself. One day in the uptown grammar school might be better than a thousand in the downtown community school. And the more legitimate on theoretical grounds it becomes to have such community schools, the more the actual differences in life-chance between the priority area children and the others will be overlooked. If equality is really what we are after, then the obvious view must also be the correct one, that it is more conducive to equality for people to study roughly the same things at school than radically different things.

This obvious view can itself be defended in two somewhat different ways. On the one hand there may be an argument from justice. It is assumed that the traditional curriculum is a good; and it is then argued that to offer this good to some children and not to others is a manifest injustice. This, in crude summary, is the argument put forward by Denis Lawton in his book, *Class, Culture and the Curriculum* (Routledge and Kegan Paul, 1975). The basic theory upon which his argument rests is that it is possible to 'separate political-economic differences and conflicts in society from questions about its cognitive and cultural basis'. If this separation is made, then it is possible, he thinks, to sort out what knowledge and what cultural inheritance is good. This done, he has then considered the question of a common curriculum as a question about fair distribution, and, relying on a Rawlsian definition of justice, has argued (p. 116) that 'pupils should have access to the same kind of curriculum unless good reasons can be shown for providing different curricula. The onus is on those who wish to provide different curricula to demonstrate that this will be "fair" ' and this he thinks his opponents have failed to do.

But it is obvious on further inspection that Lawton's argument is not really about equality at all. His proof that there should be a common curriculum is really based on the belief that some sorts of curricula are worth pursuing and others are less good. He can then go on to raise the question whether it is right to deny this good to any section of society. So perhaps what we have here is not a direct rebuttal of the Midwinter argument but something different.

The other kind of defence of the obvious view (namely that egalitarianism demands a common syllabus) is somewhat different. It turns on the point that any kind of distinction institutionally drawn between one pupil and another, whether by placing some in different schools, streaming them according to ability, or examining them within different systems of examinations, is itself anti-egalitarian. And this is manifestly true. The conclusion drawn on this theory is that a system must be devised so flexible that it can be made to accommodate everyone, whatever his ability, whatever his cultural background. One curriculum for all is thus advocated, but a curriculum which is genuinely suitable for all, not one suitable only for the middle-class or most academic. Midwinter's argument for diversification of curriculum turned on the point that a common curriculum was absolutely bound to favour the middle-class child, and thus to doom the working-class to failure. Lawton's argument against him was that the common curriculum, whether middle-class or not, could be shown to be a good from which no one ought to be excluded. The new argument is that it is possible to devise a curriculum which is both common and non-middle class, adaptable for all, and within which no one is doomed to failure or frustration.

The Schools Council paper advocating a common examination for all children at sixteen-plus can be regarded as an attempt at such a defence (*Examinations at 16+. Proposals for the Future*, Schools Council, 1976). Is is a rather confused document, in that part of its motivation seemed to be to save schools from the administrative expense and inconvenience of administering two examinations (G.C.E. and C.S.E.) at the same time. There is therefore quite a lot of argument from convenience in the paper. But here and there the egalitarian argument in favour of unity of examination can be picked out; and unified examination could be taken to entail a unified curriculum. The authors speak, for instance, of 'the recognition of children's abilities as forming a continuum within which it is neither possible nor desirable to make rigid divisions into separate categories'. The new single curriculum would have to be such as to provide 'valid goals' for the majority of all children at school; otherwise it would not be fair. Here, then, is the proposal for a common curriculum, within which there will be common syllabuses and common examinations for all of the top sixty per cent of children in schools. (It is always allowed sometimes tacitly, sometimes explicitly, that those who have been designated 'handicapped' may have a different curriculum. Lawton would presumably argue that their handicap provides a valid reason for excluding them from the common culture which the rest, in justice must share in. The Schools Council might argue that such children are so manifestly in need of special treatment that they cannot be harmed by discrimination.) In the Schools Council paper there is, understandably, nothing about the content of the common curriculum; that was not what the paper was about. But the arguments do in a way constitute an answer to Midwinter. For it is true that according to these proposals, children will not be educated so that they must fail, or only the bottom forty per cent will be so educated. For no one will fail. Everyone will just do his best in the continuum of ability. But we still do not know what they will actually learn.

It seems, then, that there is no way in which we can derive any answers to the question what ought to be taught at school from considerations of equality. We have seen that egalitarianism has led some to suggest different curricula geared to the environment and culture of the child; but just as strongly the same egalitarianism had led in the other more natural direction, to the view that children at school should all be taught in accordance with the same curriculum. The arguments must be taken to be inconclusive. But of course by far the most important question that can be raised about education *is* the question what to teach. If notions of equality and fairness cannot provide answers to my question, it is necessary to leave such notions behind, and see if it is possible to find any solutions from other sources, employing criteria other than that of equality.

III

Curriculum Structure

We have reached the position where it seems that more important than questions about how teaching is to be carried out, or
even to whom education is to be distributed, are questions about
what is to be taught in schools. And at this point it is necessary
to raise again one of the central questions of this book: to what
extent are our decisions political? For considerations of equality
have been shown to be inadequate to settle questions of curriculum, whether at school or indeed at university. And so our task
must be to examine other criteria by which to establish or
criticize curricula. But are these criteria purely educational? Are
there in fact any *purely* educational considerations by which to
settle such questions, or are all the criteria we may think of
really political, just as political as the criterion of equality was,
though perhaps more disguisedly so?

Obviously we are entering here on very difficult territory, for
we seem to need some clear way of distinguishing the political
from the non-political, and such clarity may not be forthcoming. At this stage, perhaps it is enough to issue a general warning
against some of the more manifest confusions which may arise.

It is often assumed that if a judgement can be shown to contain some element of evaluation, then it is a political judgement.
Now passing judgement on different proposals, or making
decisions of policy between one proposal and another, must
obviously contain elements of evaluation, or at least must be
capable of being justified by value judgements, by explanations
of what is being preferred to what. But such judgements need
not necessarily therefore be properly described as political,

although they may be used politically in some circumstances. For the distinction between value judgements and political decisions is that the latter are concerned with public policy and thus with power, power to affect the freedom of persons other than those who are making the evaluation. An instance of a political decision would be a decision about how to raise money from people (by taxation, loan or levy) and then how much of this money to spend on items which have been independently assessed as good. So it might be agreed that a certain kind of education was good, and this in itself, though involving evaluation, would not yet be a political decision. But the decision to spend public money on this kind of education, or how much money to spend, *would* be political. The class of value judgements is wider than the class of political decisions. But of course the two classes overlap and interlock.

Thus we must avoid the assumption that any judgement whatever of the form 'it is best to do so and so' is necessarily political. The temptation to assume this may partly arise from a further assumption of a sociological kind, namely that value judgements are determined by social class. This combined with a yet further assumption that class conflict is the dynamism of society, and is itself political, leads to the equating of value with political judgements.

But such general remarks will not go far towards making the distinctions that we want. The best way to approach an answer to the question is perhaps to consider ways in which it has been proposed in the past to justify, establish or perpetuate curricula of education, and to see how far claims that such arguments were purely educational could be upheld. There can be no objection to saying, tautologically, that to justify a curriculum *on educational grounds* is to claim that one who follows it will end up an educated person; that one who followed only half of it, or a different curriculum altogether, would be less well educated; and that there are some objects of study which might have nothing educational to recommend them, are of no educational value. Even at this stage we do not need, I believe, to concern ourselves with definitions of education, provided

Curriculum Structure

that we are clear that education is generally thought of as good. From this it obviously follows that when we discuss what an educational curriculum should contain, we are looking for elements which it is good to know, elements which are, that is to say, constitutive of the overall good which being educated is. The question is, therefore, not whether those who advocate this or that as part of a curriculum think it is good to know this or that (for so much can be taken for granted) but rather whether their judgement that it is so is a political judgement, or can be justified on other grounds.

With these preliminaries behind us, then, let us look at some of the arguments that have been used in the past to justify specific educational curricula. We may conveniently and conventionally begin by going back once again to Plato. If we consider in more detail the educational proposals contained in Plato's *Republic*, it is because we are now in a position to see plainly, more than before, what are the assumptions which lie behind his proposals, and how extraordinarily different in some ways they are from our own. And this may have more than historical or curiosity value; it may be a way of forcing us to consider our own assumptions, and how we would justify *them*.

Plato assumes, to start off with, that the purpose of education is to acquire knowledge, and that knowledge is very difficult to acquire, and therefore not everyone will be fitted by nature to acquire it. Some may be simply incapable of the intellectual exercises to be gone through. But he also has no doubt that to have knowledge is better than not to have it, and that it is worth having for its own sake. Consider the famous passage at the beginning of Book Seven of the *Republic*, where, in introducing the discussion of the educational curriculum for the élite, he uses the allegory of the Cave. In the allegory, people who are not educated are represented as prisoners in a cave, tied up in such a way that they can look only at a blank screen, on which various shadows appear. These shadows are cast by figures, statues and other things, carried along behind a wall and projecting over the top of it, and lighted by a fire high up in the cave behind the prisoners' backs. The only sounds the prisoners hear, apart from their own voices, are echoes which seem to come from the screen, but which are really produced by the voices of the statue-bearers, from behind the wall. The prisoners think that the shadows and the echoes are real, because they are facing the wrong way to see or hear what is actually going on. The process of education is the long and painful process which begins whenever a prisoner breaks his bonds and turns to face the other way. Then he sees the real people, carrying the statutes, and he begins to understand what it is that he has been seeing and hearing up to now, even though at first he is dazzled by the fire-light and cannot see the real objects properly, finding it easier to turn back and look at the shadows of the real. The educational process continues with the prisoner being dragged reluctantly out of the cave altogether and into the sunlight above. Once again, at this stage, his eyes are dazzled and he cannot see anything at all. But when he becomes accustomed to the light, he understands that reality is what goes on above the cave, and he both begins to despise what goes on below, and to be in fact less competent at discriminating the shadows, if he temporarily goes down among his former colleagues. But he no longer wants to go back and compete with the prisoners. 'If he is reminded of his previous life, and of what passed for wisdom then, and of his fellow prisoners, don't you think he will deem himself happy in the change, and feel pity for the others?' (*Republic*, 516c). In fact he would welcome any fate, and accept any position, however lowly, in the real world rather than go back to the cave.

In expounding the meaning of this allegory, Plato insists that education is not a matter of putting into the mind new knowledge that was not there before, or of giving a new power of sight to eyes previously blind. It is rather a matter of turning the eyes or the mind in the right direction. To educate a man you must turn his mind away from the things which are not proper objects of knowledge, towards those which are, and this will be a painful and tedious process.

Now this picture makes no sense at all unless there is a definite and absolute criterion by which to judge which way a man is facing, whether the *wrong* way towards the shadows, or the *right* way, towards the light. Plato not only rejects the 'bucket' theory of the mind (to borrow Popper's phrase) according to which you can fill the mind with anything whatever, at will, but he also rejects any kind of relativist theory, which might suggest that that *counts as* knowledge which the mind happens to accept or to have fed into it. The prisoners think that they have knowledge before their enlightenment, but they are mistaken. It is not a matter of opinion, but a matter of fact.

Let us now pursue Plato's theory a bit further, and follow him into his curriculum-planning after the allegory has been left behind. Leaving the cave and coming up into the light of the real world represents leaving the world of concrete particular objects and coming out, though gradually, into the world of the abstract and general. This is the only proper object of knowledge, in Plato's view. Thus a good education will necessarily be an education which leads its participants to a familiarity with abstract ideas. True education must consist in turning the pupil's attention away from particular examples and individual, concrete experiences towards general and abstract truths.

Plato believed in a world of Forms, permanent objects of knowledge called by such names as Whiteness-in-itself, Goodness-in-itself and so on. That is the first thing we learn about Plato, and very extraordinary it sounds. However, it seems to me that if one concentrates too much upon the detached and mysterious nature of the Platonic Forms one may tend to reject the Platonic doctrine of education as too esoteric or bizarre to merit serious enlightened consideration. I do not believe that if we refuse to tangle with questions such as 'What did Plato think the Forms were? Where did he think they existed?' we are being unfair. Rather the reverse. One has to remember that in writing about the Forms he was not only exploring new thoughts, but trying to make the exceptionally concrete Greek language express things it had never expressed before. And if the language refused, if the words would not mean what he wanted them to mean without ambiguities and unwanted implications, this is not to be wondered at. Let us therefore not try to understand the ramifications of the theory of Forms as such, but simply for our purposes follow the theory of education where it leads.

The theory leads firmly in the direction of knowledge of the abstract and general rather than the concrete and particular. Arithmetic is first introduced as that earliest part of the curriculum which is 'Παρακλήτικον' (parakletikon), which calls in the mind, that is to say, to solve problems which the senses alone cannot solve (523b). 'Some things that we perceive do not call in the help of the understanding to examine them, because they can be settled well enough by perception on its own; but others cry out for the understanding, because perception gives no sound result.' Perception on its own, when it comes to concepts of number, will always give contradictory results. One cannot, by merely looking at something, decide whether to count it as one thing or as a number of component different things, any more than one can decide whether to ascribe to it one relative property like 'large' or the opposite. So, Plato argues, the whole *general* idea of what counts as one thing, what as many, what a unit of counting is, has to be explored. And this is the abstract science of number. The great merit of studying this subject is not that it solves any particular puzzles about the perceived world, still less that it helps one to calculate for business or professional purposes (though it may incidentally have both these advantages). It is rather that it leads one inevitably to more and further abstractions. Now this kind of education is difficult, and if one becomes good at it, one will become good at thinking as a whole; but, far more important, learning about abstract properties is learning the truth, and this is good in itself.

The next subject in the curriculum, which he holds to be next in some orderly progression of complexity, is geometry. And for this he claims similar advantages; then comes solid geometry, then astronomy (the study of solid bodies in motion), then harmony. Each of these subjects is to be studied not empirically but entirely in the abstract. Even astronomy and harmony are to be treated as branches of mathematics, and any consideration of actual planets or actual sounds is to be discouraged. The movements of the stars and the sounds of the strings are simply a source of examples. All the subjects in the curriculum must finally be seen to be linked in their mathematical nature, in the truths which they contain (531d). 'If this brings us to the position where the subjects are linked and related to each other and to a conclusion about what they have in common, then the work takes us towards our goal, and is worth the labour.'

It is the nature of knowledge itself, what counts as true knowledge, and what the only proper objects of knowledge are which, in Plato's view, is bound to dictate the content of the educational curriculum, and to dictate even the order in which it is to be followed. The end result will be a kind of synoptic view of everything that can be known, with an understanding of what is and what is not worth pursuing, in general.

It is obvious that, from our point of view, the curriculum which Plato argues for is hopelessly narrow and one-sided. It contains no history, no art; literature is quite explicitly ruled out, and even natural science is totally non-empirical and abstract. It is in fact an education in nothing but mathematics and number-theory. But the simplicity of the scheme and the single-minded nature of the arguments for it make it a good, because pure, specimen of the *educational* defence of a curriculum. The purpose of education is to give people knowledge and there is no real knowledge except mathematical knowledge. But of course, notoriously, the argument, though initially purely educational or epistemological, has a political conclusion. As we saw on page 17, the distinction between the 'educational' and the 'political' cannot really be maintained, in Plato's view of the matter. For the synoptic view which is the final goal of education will bring understanding not only of mathematics in all its branches but also, mysteriously, of what is good and what is bad, in areas quite non-mathematical. This is not because mathematical thinking will make people good at decision making, but because the objects of knowledge—the Forms, are *both* mathematical and, at the same time, ethical. So educated men are uniquely fit to enter government and make decisions on behalf of other members of society, since only they know what is good and what is bad.

93

Thus only the educated can properly govern. But education is, as Plato insists, difficult; and not everyone is capable of it. So only those naturally fit to govern will be educated, only those, that is, who come of the proper stock, and who have the natural capabilities necessary for following the mathematical curriculum. So there are two crucial points at which political considerations enter the 'pure' arguments about curriculum content. First, the system is élitist, because the content of the curriculum is intrinsically selective. It would simply be impossible for just anybody to understand it. Secondly, it is taken to be a matter of fact that the completion of the curriculum entails a kind of knowledge necessary for the proper exercise of power. The only reason why the defence of this particular curriculum could be conducted on educational grounds is that, not Plato alone, but Greeks in general believed that true knowledge must be abstract, and *also* that being a good man (and therefore a good leader of men) entailed having knowledge. Putting these two (to us astonishing) beliefs together, you reach the Platonic conclusion that you only have to fix a curriculum of education which maximizes abstract knowledge and to confine it to those people fit to follow it, to ensure a government maximally good.

So much, then, for Plato's 'pure' educational arguments for a particular and specific curriculum content. They are fascinating arguments, but we cannot conceivably employ them ourselves. For we share neither Plato's belief in the essentially abstract nature of knowledge, nor his belief in the superiority of the intellect (the organ of knowledge) over all other human attributes. Even if we thought the mathematician superior to everyone else in intellect, we would be reluctant to conclude that he was superior to everyone else in general (just, absolutely, without qualification, superior), and therefore uniquely fit to wield power.

However, even if we abandon Plato, there are other quite different possibilities. His is not the only attempt at a 'pure' justification of a curriculum. Some purely educational justifications for a particular kind of curriculum have been based on the concept of the natural growth and development of the pupil, a tradition of curriculum-building deriving perhaps ultimately from Rousseau. Such theories are bound to concentrate on broad outlines of kinds of learning appropriate to children. It follows that they cannot give so much detailed attention to the *outcome* of the process, and therefore they are less likely to come up with specific answers to the question of what should be taught. For if the emphasis is on growth, it is less easy to place a limit on this process. So such theorists do not concern themselves much to say what the educated man should finally know.

Another, non-Platonic attempt to answer the crucial question of curriculum content on grounds which are, like Plato's, supposed to be epistemological or 'pure', is to be found in the theories of Paul Hirst, now conveniently brought together in one book of selected articles (*Knowledge and the Curriculum*, Routledge and Kegan Paul, 1974). Hirst's doctrines, though not necessarily wholly original, have not only been widely discussed but actually used, often without discussion, by such persons as the constructors of new courses at polytechnics. The expression, 'forms of knowledge' central to his theory, is frequently and widely employed in such contexts; moreover R. S. Peters, in his introduction to Hirst's book (*Op. cit.*, p. viii) has said that 'there is a sense in which anyone working in the field has to take up some stand with regard to the "forms of knowledge" '. One should not contemplate disobedience to such a call.

The first essay in which the forms of knowledge were introduced was entitled 'Liberal Education and the Nature of Knowledge' and was published in 1965. The notion of a liberal education is that of an education which is not vocational, but is considered as intrinsically valuable. It is one justifiable, therefore, on 'educational' rather than on political or other extraneous grounds. Thus the whole of Hirst's discussion takes place on the assumption that there can be such 'pure' justifications for at least some educational curricula. The only question to be answered is what are the grounds for such a justification, or what are the criteria by which items of the liberal curriculum are to be judged fit or unfit for inclusion. Ever since the days of Plato, Hirst says, the basis for the values that should determine education has been 'located in man's conception of the diverse forms of knowledge he has achieved'. He does not dissent from this location. He says (p. 38) 'a consistent concept of liberal education must be worked out fully in terms of the forms of knowledge'. If such a basis for the planning of a curriculum is employed, the mind of the person following the curriculum will (incidentally) be developed, since, on Hirst's view, to talk of the development of the mind is only another way of talking about the acquisition of knowledge: there is a logical connexion between the two, 'the achievement of knowledge is necessarily the development of mind . . . that is the self-conscious rational mind of man . . . in its most fundamental aspect'. The rest of the discussion is therefore carried on primarily in terms of knowledge, but the developmental, or Rousseauesque, view is not explicitly rejected.

What, then, are the forms of knowledge? First of all we are warned against thinking of them as 'collections of information'. Rather they are 'the complex ways of understanding experience which man has achieved, which are publicly specifiable and which are gained through learning' (p. 38). Each different form of knowledge, we are told, involves the development of thinking, communicating and so on 'in ways that are peculiar to itself as a way of understanding experience'. And examples are offered; knowing how to solve problems in Euclidean geometry, knowing how to understand the poems of John Donne, these would be different forms of knowledge.

Now it must be admitted that so far the ideas, though vaguely, are not precisely intelligible, or so it seems to me. Perhaps the difficulty lies in what it is that Hirst thinks constitutes knowledge in general. For he does not define knowledge in terms of truth. He does not, that is, think of knowledge as that which could be expressed in true propositions. To adopt this line would be to take up what seems to him an unduly 'realist' view. Instead he tries to define knowledge in terms of 'testable assertions' constructed out of symbols which give public embodiment to concepts, themselves part of a shared conceptual schema (p. 39). The point here is that the assertions have to be testable, that is, such that they *can* be tested. And they will fulfil this condition if the language in which they are expressed is understood. This language will be understood only if it symbolizes, in a recognized way, concepts which are public. Such a set of concepts is sometimes referred to as a 'conceptual framework'. So knowledge is defined *first* in terms of meaning, and *secondarily* in terms of truth.

Learning to use the symbols in which meaningful assertions can be made is, presumably, to put it briefly, learning the language. So there must be a language which can be learned before there can be any knowledge. To this we can readily agree. But so far, Hirst seems only to have pointed to the conditions necessary for there to be knowledge; he has not told us much about how to distinguish what is knowledge from what is not (for bogus claims to knowledge would also be uttered in *some language or other*, and, if they were to be at all plausible, would be uttered in the very same language as the true claim) Nor has he told us how to distinguish one *form* of knowledge from another. This last omission must be remedied, if the curriculum is to be constructed out of the different forms that there are.

Let us turn once more to his actual words to see if we can get help. Summing up his position in the middle of his article he writes (p. 43): 'It is a necessary feature of knowledge as such that there be *public criteria whereby the true is distinguishable from the false* [my italics]. . . . It is the existence of these criteria which gives objectivity to knowledge; and this in its turn gives objectivity to the concept of liberal education.' Thus, if we teach people the criteria, we are educating them, that is, giving them knowledge. The next step is to distinguish the forms; and each form, he repeats is 'a distinct way in which our experience becomes structured round the use of accepted public symbols'. We can distinguish one form from another, then, by distinguishing *one distinct set of symbols from another*. Hirst lists four ways in which this can be done:

(1) There are, quite simply, different words, or concepts central to each. For example, 'gravity' and 'photosynthesis' are scientific

concepts, while 'God' is religious and 'right' is moral. But so far this is not really much help. How fine should our distinctions be? Are 'gravity' and 'photosynthesis', for instance, parts of one (scientific) vocabulary or of two vocabularies, those of physics and biology? Is 'sonnet' a part of a different set of concepts from 'sonata', or are both parts of one 'artistic' set? The second rule for distinguishing symbols into sets may help:

(2) In a given form of knowledge, we are told, the concepts form a network of possible relationships in which experience can be understood. So the words within each set should be, if not mutually inter-definable, at least mutually explanatory, or capable of being related. The vagueness of this test is perhaps no fatal disadvantage. If you thought, in general, that the notion of a sonnet could be explained without reference to concepts such as 'right' or 'God', this would put 'sonnet' into a separate class, but would not debar you from explaining a particular sonnet by reference to the idea of God. This last would be a case where the forms of religious and literary knowledge crossed.

(3) The third rule simply restates the conditions already laid down for knowledge in general. 'The form, by virtue of its particular terms and logic has expressions . . . that in some way or other . . . are testable against experience.'

(4) Finally in the fourth rule, we are told that each separate form has developed its own particular skills and techniques for exploring experience and testing the truth of the relevant propositions.

Summing up the rules, and acknowledging certain areas of haziness and overlap, Hirst says (p. 45): 'The central feature to which they point is that the major forms of knowledge, or disciplines, can each be distinguished by their dependence on some particular kind of test against experience for their distinctive expressions.' He then goes on to list the empirical sciences (which depend, he says, on observational tests), mathematics (which depends on deductive demonstrations from axioms) and, rather cavalierly he lists separately moral knowledge, the arts, historical knowledge, religious knowledge and the human sciences. But in the case of all these he is cautious in characterizing precisely the kind of 'test against experience' which the expressions in each should be subject to. Apart from these seven forms of knowledge Hirst says that there can also be distinguished certain fields of knowledge, held together 'simply by their subject matter' but not 'concerned to validate any one logically distinct form of expression'. An example of such a field is geography; another is legal studies. The principle of curriculum-building is then finally enunciated: it is to ensure that everybody has some knowledge of every possible form. 'What is being sought is first sufficient immersion in the concepts, logic and criteria of the discipline for a person to come to know the distinctive way in which it "works" by pursuing these in particular cases; and then sufficient generalization of these over the whole range of the discipline so that his experience begins to be widely structured in this distinctive manner. It is this coming to look at things in a certain way that is being aimed for. . . . It is the ability to recognize empirical assertions or aesthetic judgements for what they are and to know the kind of criteria on which their validity depends that matter' (p. 47). And he concludes (p. 48): 'A liberal education approached directly in terms of the disciplines will thus be composed of the study of at least paradigm examples of all the various forms of knowledge.'

It has been necessary to quote Hirst's original article at some length in order to try to understand exactly what he is advocating as the method of building up, by reference to educational considerations alone, a whole curriculum, the pursuit of which will produce an educated man. We must notice again his unwillingness to say that education is a matter of learning the truth. To say this would imply that there *was* a truth which could be taught and learned, and to this simple view he does not adhere. Instead he claims that education is a matter of learning a language, which is common and public, and within which it is possible to say things which are true *or* false, and things which make sense *or* nonsense. He frequently speaks of criteria by which this language is tested against experience, but is somewhat shifting in his approach to the question what the testing is for. Is it for truth? or for coherence? Is it for 'validity'? or for adequacy? This is left unclear. (Elsewhere, in his essay 'The Contribution of Philosophy' (in *Changing the Curriculum*, edited by J. F. Kerr, University of London Press, 1968), Hirst has explicitly identified meaningfulness with truth in respect of testability. 'Types of meaning can only be classified along with types of claim to truth. Realms of meaning become distinct when we find different types of claims to knowledge', but he goes on somewhat confusingly to add, as examples of claims to knowledge, the claims made 'when there are principles by which we can distinguish truth from error, right from wrong, beautiful from ugly and so on'.) What is to be understood is that each different form of knowledge has a different language, with its own logic; and that each language will contain certain keywords in its vocabulary. So just as you can tell whether it is Latin or Greek you are studying by seeing whether the word 'felicitas' or the word 'εὐδαιμονία' (eudaimonia) crops up on the page, so presumably you can tell whether it is biology or music by seeing whether the word 'cell' or 'symphony' crops up more frequently in the discussion. You are supposed to be able to recognize that such words form parts of radically different vocabularies. So far this may be reasonable enough. But is this recognition really possible, except on the assumption that we can already distinguish one subject from another? And, if that is the prior requisite, how are we supposed to do that? If called on to explain how we knew that 'cell' and 'symphony' formed parts of different languages, would we not be inclined to say that the only sense in which they did so was the sense in which biology was different from music; and if asked what *that* sense was, we might say that in finding out about biology we would be concerned with different things from the things that would concern us in music.

This is certainly in part what Hirst means. There have indeed been many other exponents of distinctions rather like the forms of knowledge who have not used the word 'language' at all in drawing their distinctions, but have spoken instead of 'concepts', 'modes of experience', 'ways of knowledge' or have used still other expressions. But the idea of different sets of symbols, of different languages and their supposedly related different logics has gained such currency in discussions of curriculum that it is perhaps necessary to pursue it a little further. R. S. Peters (*Op. cit.*) says: 'This general thesis [that is Hirst's] has support . . . from Wittgenstein's thesis about distinct "language games".' And there is no doubt that it is general reverence for this doctrine that makes Hirst's distinctions seem more intelligible than perhaps they are. Let us for a moment turn back, then, to Wittgenstein's original words.

First of all, it is worth noticing that part of what appealed to Wittgenstein in the use of the expression 'language-game' (*Sprachspiel*) was the extreme variety of things which can all be called 'games' (and *Spiel* is perhaps even more varied). So there is not going to be only one sort of language-game. There will be only a family resemblance between different language games as between other kinds of game (and the notion of a game was that with which Wittgenstein introduced the whole subject of family resemblance). The point of using the joint expression then is partly to suggest how many different kinds of languages there could be. But the expression also emphasizes that a language does not consist in words alone, but in words uttered in a particular context, used as part of a particular communal communicative activity, a form of life, as Wittgenstein put it. In the famous paragraph 23 of the *Philosophical Investigations*, he says: 'There are . . . countless different kinds of use of what we call "symbols", "words", "sentences". And this multiplicity is not something fixed, given once and for all; but new types of language, new language-games as we may say, come into existence, and others become obsolete and get forgotten. . . . Here the term language-*game* is meant to bring into prominence the fact that the *speaking* of language is part of an activity, or of a form of life.'

The main point of distinguishing one language-game from another is to enable a philosopher to draw certain further distinctions; to show, for example, when an expression is being taken to belong to one language-game, though it is really being uttered in another. For instance one may wrongly think that the expression of pain, or even the statement that one is experiencing a sensation such as pain, belongs to the same game as the ascription to something of a characteristic for which there are criteria of applicability. When there is this kind of crossing of language-game barriers the result is philosophical confusion. But in spite of his insistence that we may wrongly assume an expression to have been uttered as part of one game when it really belongs to another, Wittgenstein does not actually tell us how to distinguish one from another. Understandably he does not give a definition of 'language-game', any more than he would be willing to give a definition, to state a common central meaning, of 'game'. We just have to pick up the differences between one and another as we go along. We just *know*, if we know the language, both that all the different instances of games are properly called games, and that they are different from one another. So with language-games we get examples which are supposed to be *manifestly* different: 'Review the multiplicity of language-games in the following examples, and in others:

Giving orders and obeying them . . .

Describing the appearance of an object, or giving its measurements

. . . Play-acting, singing catches, guessing riddles and so on.' (*Op. cit.*, para. 23.)

And again: 'Think of exclamations alone, with their completely different functions, Away!, Water!, Ow!, Help!, Fine!, No! Are you still inclined to call these words "names of objects"?' (*Op. cit.*, para. 27.) So the difficulty which we found with regard to Hirst's different sets of symbols crops up again with regard to language-games themselves. How do we know they are different? Being told that each is part of a different form of life does not help. For we cannot, except by the same intuitive understanding, distinguish these either.

Perhaps we shall be better off if we consider the different 'logics' or 'grammar' which Hirst says belong to different sets of symbols. For a different logic has, presumably a different set of rules, different standards by which to judge self-contradiction, consistency, entailment and so on. But here there is no help either. For though it is characteristic of a language, as of a game, to be based upon rules, the rules are co-extensive with the language and cannot be defined in terms of anything else, outside the language. 'Grammar does not tell us how language must be constructed in order to fulfil its purpose, in order to have such-and-such an effect on human beings. It only describes and in no way explains the use of signs. The rules of grammar may be called "arbitrary" if that is to mean that the *aim* of grammar is nothing but that of the language. If someone says "If our language had not this grammar, it could not express these facts" it should be asked what "could" means here.' (Wittgenstein, *Philosophical Investigations*, I, para. 496, 497.) What is true of language in general is true of particular language-games as well. The logic, the set of rules of the game, has no point except the point of the game. The rules merely describe, they do not explain, the game.

What does it really mean, then, to say that one form of knowledge is to be distinguished from another by the logic and the language it employs? Wittgenstein, in speaking of different language-games, was making a point about language and meaning, not about the forms of life he thought were expressed in different language-games. Hirst, on the other hand, in speaking of different languages, is attempting to make a point about the different forms of knowledge to which these languages belong. If he wants to show, as he does, that a curriculum must be built up so as to include different forms of knowledge, he must find some way of demonstrating what these different forms of knowledge are, other than by just saying that each employs a different language. In so far as he does say this he certainly gets no support from the *Philosophical Investigations*, whatever Peters may suggest to the contrary.

After all, if we think, to take one of Wittgenstein's examples, that to say 'I feel cold' is to describe something, we may get into familiar philosophical difficulties about how we know, and how other people know, that what we say is true. Muddling different language-games has philosophical consequences, and the point of introducing the notion of different 'games' was to suggest that we shall come to philosophical harm, a dead end, if we do not face the fact that different 'games' are truly different and cannot be assimilated. But this penalty has no analogue in the case of the different 'languages' allegedly employed in the different forms of knowledge. If I persist in speaking of musical tonality in terms properly belonging to biology, I shall fail to make myself understood, at best be thought to be indulging in a baroque and bewildering kind of metaphor. Quite independently of a comparison of the languages used, we know that music and biology are different. Not only do we know them to be different, but we may want to suggest that both should be taught at school—this is a separate point. Hirst, in the same way, may well have excellent reasons for suggesting that both subjects should be included in the school curriculum, but he ought not to pretend that he can demonstrate that this is desirable by reference to a set of rules, a logic, a grammar or a language for each. He both fails to distinguish the subjects, and *also* fails to demonstrate their desirable nature, by his practice. And such a practice may not only be unilluminating, it may be positively misleading. For it may suggest an inevitability, a necessity, for distinguishing one subject from another which is not in fact to be found. The words 'logic', and 'language' as well, sound powerful and authoritative barriers by which to fence one thing off from another.

Perhaps part of what Hirst was aiming at was to ensure that he could find reasons for people at school becoming acquainted with *something* of all the subjects which he thought, on independent grounds, that it was desirable for them to know about. And this may have suggested the terminology of the 'language'. For if you learn a real language, such as French, you can gradually get the hang of it, and then you are enabled to go on with it, and read more and understand more if you want to. It is not necessary to read all of French literature at school; you can continue to do this for yourself provided you have the essentials of the language at your command. So Hirst may, understandably, have had in mind that if the basics of a subject could only be taught, then pupils would have the option of going ahead with the subject if they wanted to. This could be the source of the metaphor of the language.

But if so, though one may sympathize with the ideal, there is a fundamental objection to the metaphor itself. For it is not at all easy to discover what would count as the basic tool, the language, of a scientific subject, or of history, still less of literature or music. There is no way of teaching techniques, short of teaching the subject itself. Teaching people how to think scientifically *is* teaching them some science. They have to understand the subject matter, know a number of the scientific *facts*, before they can possibly understand a particular 'mode of thought'. One cannot stand at one remove and learn how mathematicians think without actually getting down to doing mathematics. There is no such thing as understanding the 'form' of knowledge involved in playing the French horn, except in so far as one knows how to play the horn. A general view of what was common to the playing of the horn, the piano and the violin would hardly give one much knowledge, any more than would a general view of what was common to physics, botany and biochemistry. The supposition that you may concentrate on one branch of science or of music and take this as a specimen of 'scientific thought' or 'musical expertise' does not make much sense. What is the *extra* point in taking it as a specimen or an example? What *more* have you learned by so taking it than you would have learned anyway? Of course it may well be true that in teaching, for instance, history, you are teaching historical method. But in order to teach historical method you have to teach history, not methodology. There is a danger, to which we shall return, that, on the Hirst theory of the curriculum, pupils will always be concerned with second-order subjects, what is supposed to lie behind the subject (to be common to it and other parts of that 'form') while of what lies in front they remain in ignorance.

But in discussing Hirst (and by implication all those who have followed him in wishing to construct the curriculum so as to preserve or exemplify different forms of knowledge) we have inadvertently slipped into the discussion of the curriculum as divided up in traditional style into different subjects; and it has of course been frequently suggested that Hirst's arguments for the forms of knowledge are, though greatly dressed up, really conservative arguments for old-fashioned subjects as they already exist in schools and universities, in the preservation of which teachers have a vested interest. As we have seen already in Chapter II, there are numerous ways in which the attack on subjects can be launched, some radical, some less so. In the general context of an examination of criteria for the choice of curriculum-content it is necessary to look again briefly at these attacks, and at the alternatives to 'subjects' which are suggested.

Perhaps the most radical form of the attack is the sociological argument, best known in England through the writings of Michael Young and those essayists who are represented in his collection *Knowledge and Control* (Collier-Macmillan, 1971). The sociological attack on traditional subjects, unlike Hirst's own arguments, cannot be categorized finally as educational or as political. And of course it would be surprising if it could, since its authors are confident that *all* arguments, and especially all arguments about education, are political. The question which Michael Young raises is that of the 'social basis for different subjects'. What is to be included in the school curriculum is chosen and organized by those who are in power. It is power which determines what shall count as knowledge as well as determining the methods of passing on this knowledge, and the nature of the groups to whom it shall be passed on. 'Academic curricula in this country', he writes (*Op. cit.*, p. 34), 'involve assumptions that some kinds and areas of knowledge are much more "worth-while" than others: that as soon as possible all knowledge should become specialized and with minimum explicit emphasis on the relations between the subjects specialized in and between the specialist teachers involved. It may be useful then to view curricular changes as involving changing definitions of knowledge along one or more of the dimensions towards a less or more stratified specialized and open organization of knowledge. Further that as we assume some patterns of social relations associated with any curriculum, these changes will be resisted in so far as they are perceived to undermine the values, relative power and privileges of the dominant groups involved.' The actual content of the curriculum, he goes on to say, is ordered hierarchically, the high-status subjects showing more markedly than the lower the characteristics of emphasis on written presentation, abstraction, and unrelatedness (that is, the characteristic of 'being at odds with the way people normally think').

All this takes us back to the arguments about equality in the methods of teaching which we looked at in the previous chapter. But I want now to pick out the specifically 'epistemological' aspect of Young's argument. For he is saying not only that teachers, for reasons of power and prestige, choose to distance themselves and their knowledge from their pupils, but also that, for the same reasons, they decide what shall count as knowledge. We should contrast Plato's view of education, undoubtedly hierarchic, with that outlined by Young. Plato held that only the élite would advance to knowledge; but that knowledge, recognized as such, is the indisputable goal of education. Young, on the other hand, is suggesting that there is no answer to the question what should 'count as knowledge' and therefore be a fit subject to be taught. All answers are relative to the position in society of the teacher.

Here, then, we have a plain statement of belief in the relativity of knowledge. There is of course, and has always been, a large number of different forms which epistemological relativism may take. 'Man the measure of all things' is by no means a new doctrine. But in current educational thinking, the sociological relativism represented by Young is perhaps the most potent version. In order to consider it critically, it is necessary to attempt an account of what knowledge is and is not, in general, although it may seem a simple-minded thing to attack such a theory in the context of one chapter of one book. However, it must be done. For if creeping relativism is not rooted out, then it seems to me that educationalists might as well shut up shop. Not only in theory but in practice as well, relativism tends to sap the confidence of curriculum makers and teachers; and rightly. For confidence in their own curriculum would be nothing but a sign of dogmatism, according to the theory.

What does it mean, then, to say that teachers *determine what is to count as knowledge?* (whether or not this determination depends upon their position in society can be treated as a subsequent question). A clear statement of the view in question, though presented in a negative way, is to be found in Geoffrey Esland's contribution to Michael Young's collection ('Teaching and Learning as the Organization of Knowledge', *Op. cit.*, p. 70). He defends relativism by attacking 'objectivity' in epistemology. '. . . The objectivist view of knowledge . . . is the view represented in traditional epistemology and analytic philosophy. It is also how knowledge is conceived in the reality of everyday experience where the taken for granted nature of the world is rarely questioned. The individual consciousness recognizes objects as being "out there" as coercive external realities. . . . Knowledge is thereby detached from the human subjectivity in which it is constituted, maintained and transformed. Such a view implicitly presents man as a passive receiver as the pliable socialized embodiment of external facticities. He is represented not as a world-producer but as world-produced. One finds it difficult to disagree with the claim that this epistemology is fundamentally dehumanizing. It ignores the intentionality and expressivity of human action, and the entire complex process of intersubjective negotiation of meanings. In short it disguises as given a world which has to be continually interpreted. Objectivism has been firmly embedded in the norms and rituals of academic culture and its transmission. "Bodies of knowledge" are presented for the child to learn and reproduce according to specified objective criteria.' And later, 'The curriculum is a set of arrangements of knowledge which are assumed to have a purpose. . . . Through their control of the transformations of the child's consciousness its exponents engineer theoretical world views which are thought to be valid currency in their society' (p. 84). There is a large number of different points in these quotations from Esland (and there are many other passages in the literature of open education which would make the same points) but the fundamental belief is that knowledge has been falsely represented as objective; and such representation is not only misleading but it is also a social and political weapon, since the pretence that there is such a thing as objective knowledge has been used as a means of control. So, is this belief true? Is it indeed *mis*representation to hold that knowledge is objective?

We should begin by distinguishing three kinds of knowledge, in a rough and ready way: (1) Knowledge which all members of a class, whether teachers or pupils, have of their immediate and perceived surroundings. (2) Knowledge which the teacher claims to have personally. And (3) The body of knowledge which the teacher is hired to pass on to the class. Obviously these three different aspects of knowledge interrelate and may well overlap. But they cannot all be treated in identically the same way. Let us start with (1). In the case of each one of us, and this includes children, there is a vast number of things which we know, or take for granted, about our own environment. Of much of this knowledge it is likely that, though we undoubtedly learn it, we are not taught it. Traditionally, empirical philosophers have concentrated largely on the question how we come by this knowledge; and many, such as Locke and Hume, have appeared to believe that much of it is acquired by learning *words* which name experiences: objects of sensation or thought. There is no doubt that learning language, and thus learning words with which to refer to what we experience, is a large part of the acquisition of this knowledge (which includes learning our own names and those of our families; learning that our pet is a cat, our tree a lime, that what we live in is a bungalow, or, in another sense, an area of Outstanding Natural Beauty). But besides this we also have a great deal of knowledge of a more immediately practical kind: how to get across our bedroom in the dark to turn on the light; how to get to school; how to open a tin of cat food. There is no question but that this constitutes knowledge; and it is from this kind of knowledge that we all start. Except for the mentally subnormal, who may have to be painfully taught all such things, we seem to pick up an immense amount of such knowledge in a very short time. In what sense, then is this knowledge relative (or non-objective)? And if it *is* relative, to what is it relative? For the doctrine we are considering is that *all* knowledge is non-objective; that it is all 'made' not 'given'. We are supposed to create our own worlds (or sometimes merely to interpret them), each of us for himself. However it is extremely hard to make any sense of the claim of non-objectivity with regard to this basic knowledge. If we start with the less linguistic elements of it, we would say that someone knew how to do something (for instance tie his shoelaces) only if he could do it, not just once, but more or less whenever he chose to. (Doing it just once might be a fluke: we might hesitate to say even that he *could* do it if he did it only once; and we would not say he *knew how to do it* unless he *could* do it.) It is difficult to see how such knowledge could be disputed (that is, how one could dispute that someone had it) provided that the task was completed on various occasions.

However, although many of the things taught at school are skills (knowledge of how to do things such as read or write or calculate), those who hold knowledge to be relative might say that it was not knowledge of *this* kind that they were interested in, but only knowledge of supposed facts. And these alleged facts must be such as to be expressed in words. We should move on, therefore, to the more linguistic aspects of knowledge. Here we find a certain parallel with the skills we have been considering. For it is the ability to use a word rightly on more than one occasion that is necessary before we say that a child knows a word, or knows, in some cases, what a thing is. Moreover, knowing what it is will gradually carry with it more or less further knowledge about what it is for, or what it will do, or how it will behave. A child who has a cat at home will know that it is a cat, that it is called Felix, that *being a cat* it purrs, likes fish and torments birds. A child, that is, has learned a class or general word, a name, and certain characteristics which belong to members of the class including that member named by the name. It is obviously true that what word the child learns to use in a particular context will depend upon what language he is learning to speak; and to this extent it is true, though uninteresting, that his world might have been different (to the extent that 'chat' not 'cat' might have been the word he learned to use for Felix and his kind). But we are often told something more radical than this: that he could have structured his whole world differently, that he has created the world in perceiving it and learning to classify it, and that he could have created a different world. It is this radical claim which often seems to lie behind the statement that knowledge is socially determined, not absolute; or the statement that it is contingent upon whose knowledge it is, not objective for everyone.

The claim can either mean that the child could have employed different concepts which would have divided things up and classified them differently, or that he could have understood the concept he has differently, ascribed different *meanings* to the things he observed and classified. Let us look at these two possibilities in turn. The first seems to be an extension, though an interesting one, of the thought that the child could have learned a different language. As far as natural kinds like cats and dogs go, probably most languages will have a word for most of the grossly discriminable kinds, and could easily add new words for, say, newly imported or newly distinguished creatures or artefacts. But notoriously not all languages have the same descriptive words; and if a child had been brought up learning ancient Greek instead of English as his native tongue, he would not be able to say that things were blue or pink, and therefore he could not be said to *know* that pink was the colour of the rose outside his bedroom window, or blue the colour of his pyjamas. He would not be able to say, precisely, that it was his *duty* to go to school nor that he *felt* happy (only that he felt as if he were εὐδαίμων (eudaimon), a rather different thing). There is a number of different issues involved in pointing out these comparatively interesting facts. First, even if it is true that a child might have spoken a different language, and thus might have employed certain different concepts, this does not entail that he chose what language or concepts to employ. There may be some sense in saying that I might have been brought up to speak French as my first language—after all plenty of people are —but there is no sense in saying that I *chose* to be brought up speaking English. Thus if categories and concepts are closely related to language I cannot be said to have chosen the latter any more than the former. In general, that we can conceive of having done something other than we do does not entail that we freely chose to do whatever it is we are doing. So the question of choice does not arise in the sense suggested. Obviously we may 'choose our words', but not what language it is we first learn. Moreover one must not be tempted to exaggerate the difference between one language and another. Very often the question of translatability between languages offers no difficulty at all. There is a great deal, conceptually speaking, which is common.

But how does this relate to the question of knowledge? The claim that knowledge cannot be objective seemed to rest on the claim that each of us creates the world he talks about and thus the world with regard to which he could be said to know certain facts. Thus, if language is a matter of contingency, so will facts be. What is a fact depends on what can be stated. So, if I might have used a different language, I might equally have claimed knowledge of different facts. What would *count as* a fact might have been otherwise. Here we are getting near to the radical view that teachers determine what will or will not count as a fact. Without entering upon the tangled and absolutely central philosophical question whether or not there are any categories of understanding which must necessarily be common to all humans (or all language-users or all the rational) we can say for certain that there is a limit *in practice* to the extent to which we can deliberately revise the categories we employ or the classifications we make in our assertions about the world. Nor can we deliberately revise all the attendant beliefs with regard to the permanence, spatio-temporal separateness or causal connexion of things in the world. The language we use (whichever language it is) has these beliefs to a large extent built into its structure, so that we cannot say, or understand if anyone else says, anything which contradicts these fundamental beliefs. Thus no child, coming to school equipped with the basic knowledge we have been considering, could possibly come with something absolutely structurally different from the knowledge his classmates have, or he would not be able to make the statements we are supposing that he is, as he is learning his language, able to make. Neither he nor his teacher could claim to rule out of court *all* of his claims to knowledge.

This is not of course to say that the child may not claim to know some things which the teacher will rule out. But they will be ruled out, if at all, not on the grounds that they could not constitute knowledge, but on the grounds that they are false. I shall return to this distinction in a moment, for it is obviously crucial. But first let us consider the less radical version of the non-objective view, namely, that one child may differ from another in the *interpretation* he puts on the facts, the meaning or significance he attaches to them. On this view, though categories and classifications are given, and so in a way what might count as a fact is given thereby, nevertheless what is picked out *as a fact worth claiming to know* may differ radically from one person to another. How we understand the world, what we make of it, is subjective, and is determined by factors which could be otherwise. This version of the theory obviously has some truth in it. But whatever truth it has does not really seem to support the view that knowledge cannot be objective. For when we speak, not of knowing things, but of the 'meaning' of our experience for us, we are speaking of the hold it may have on our imagination. Though we may wish to deny that the imagination is a separable 'faculty', and though it may be true that cognition and imagination merge into one another, yet there remains a point in distinguishing the two.

We are deeply interested in the different ways in which the world strikes different people, what different people see *in* the world, what they find exciting, threatening, loveable, disgusting, amusing and so on. A good teacher will both try to understand how children 'see' things, that is how they interpret them, and will also try to get the children themselves to explore this whole realm of meanings, in their own paintings, poetry and music and in that of others. Now, even though in practice what we know and how we imaginatively respond to what we know cannot be completely separated, the fact remains that they can be distinguished. The difference between the two things may constitute the difference between our private and our public life, the inner and the outer. We may struggle, perhaps all our lives, to make explicit the inner: the outer *must* to some extent be capable of being made explicit. Knowledge is, all of it, at least potentially *common* knowledge. In the sense which we are now concerned with, we cannot be said to know what cannot be stated; and statements are made to be understood by more than one person. So the theory that since each of us is affected differently by the world and interprets the world according to how it affects him cannot entail that there is no such thing as common or objective *knowledge*. Perhaps people would not have thought that it did, if they had not at the same time been over-impressed with the psychological fact that one is interested in, likely to be able easily to learn, things which touch one closely; and that these may be different for different people.

So far we have been concerned with the knowledge which children start off with, which they would claim to have, independently of anything a teacher might teach them; and we have found little support for the view that this is 'relative'. If we next consider (2), the knowledge which a teacher might personally claim to have, the case does not look so very different. Being older than his pupils he will have more; he will have classified and labelled more of his experience. But all the same considerations with regard to the system of categories or classifications he uses, and the significance he attaches to what he knows will apply to him as to his pupils. He will be no more able than they to choose from scratch what to count and what not to count as a statement of fact. But there will be one major difference. He will have become more critical than they. He will have, and be anxious to pass on to them, the crucial notion of *evidence*. As soon as he begins in conversation with his pupils to use the question 'How do you know?', he is beginning to discriminate, among the things they say, not only between the true and the false, but, more than that, between the well and the ill-supported. Now some teachers will be far more sophisticated than others in their demand for appropriate evidence to support the statements their pupils feel inclined to make. And on the degree of sophistication will to some extent depend the things which are admitted as well-supported facts and those that are ruled out. So we have come upon a sense in which it looks as if the teacher is responsible for what shall and shall not count as knowledge. For if he is sophisticated, he may say 'even if what you say is true, you can't really claim to *know* it. You tell me that Brand X washes whiter than any other brand; and it may be so. But your only evidence is the advertisement you saw last night on ITV. And that can't be taken as evidence. After all, the manufacturers would say it whether it was true or not.' In this sort of way scepticism may be induced in the pupils, not only with regard to particular propositions, but with regard to claims to knowledge in general.

But nevertheless this does not seem quite what is meant by those who say that the teacher determines what shall count as knowledge. For in the situation outlined just now, although the teacher is urging his pupils to recognize on the one hand that some statements are true, others false (which they will already know) and on the other hand that some statements are well supported and others are not (which may be less familiar to them) and finally that even true statements may be so ill supported that they should not be claimed as knowledge (a highly difficult idea to grasp), he is still operating with the assumption that *some* statements are both true and well supported and that these can be known. So though he may be inducing scepticism in his pupils (what is usually referred to as 'healthy' scepticism) he is not inducing relativism (perhaps scepticism run mad).

At this point a further complication has to be taken into account. It is obvious that the more sophisticated a teacher is, the more power he has to mislead his pupils. He may be perfectly well aware that a statement he has made is not well supported by evidence, but he may none the less present it as established fact, whether general or particular, to pupils too young and inexperienced to raise any question about evidence. But more probably a teacher will mislead his pupils through ignorance. He will himself have accepted something unquestioningly, and will pass it on in the same form to his pupils. In this sense his claims to knowledge may be false claims just as surely as may those of his pupils. So, knowingly or unknowingly, it may be he who determines what shall be counted as true. Those who say that the teacher determines what shall count as knowledge do not make it clear whether they think he does this deliberately or not (nor whether they think this matters). When they speak of teachers exerting power, imposing a hierarchy of knowledge, 'a dominant professional legitimacy' on their pupils, it sounds as if they mean that the teacher acts deliberately, even reprehensibly. At other times the teacher seems to be presented as himself a victim of the social structure, which imposes on him the *belief* in objectivity, a delusion then handed on to the pupils. The teacher is, on this view, himself deceived, and is thus an involuntary deceiver; not wicked but simple minded. Now suppose such a teacher, who begins to understand the sociology of knowledge, and whose eyes are thus opened to a new set of facts, namely that 'questions of "truth" and "validity" are also problematic' (Esland in Young, *Op. cit.*, p. 77). He may read in C. Wright Mills ('Language, Logic and Culture', *American Sociological Review*, 1939) that 'Criteria, or observational and verificatory models are not transcendental. There have been and are diverse canons and criteria of validity and truth, and these criteria, upon which determination of the truthfulness of propositions at any time depend, are themselves in their persistence and change open to socio-historical relativization.' When he reads those words, what happens to this teacher? He realizes that even his own critical use of the notion of 'good evidence' is relative to his position. Will he in future try to avoid making *any* personal claims to knowledge? He will not fear that what he claimed to know might be shown to be false, for this would presuppose criteria of truth and falsity. But he will fear that it might be senseless to make any such claim, since any criterion he might employ could be shown to be socio-historically relative.

Curriculum Structure

So the most he could say would be that what he claimed to know satisfied the criteria of well-supported truth in force for the time being. But the teacher is a practical man; and he is bound, as we all are, to make *some* claims to knowledge, even if he is cautious and likes to state as facts only those things which he believes are well supported by evidence. So it is most likely that he will simply refuse to consider relativism seriously with regard to what he personally claims to know. Is he then being dishonest? Is he conducting his life in bad faith?

Perhaps this problem matters less than one might think for the relativist theory. For the area of controversy is not what any of us may *claim to know* personally ((1) and (2) above, page 109) but about the body of knowledge which the teacher has to present to his pupils—not what *he* knows nor what *they* know, but what *is known* (or some selection of it). (Number (3) on page 109.)

Now the crucial thing, when considering this body of knowledge, is precisely to recognize that it is *not* claimed by anyone in particular, but is in a sense independent of any avowal or personal statement. Any of the 'claimed' knowledge which can be expressed in general or historical statements may be incorporated in the public body of knowledge; indeed to utter such a statement in one's own person is perhaps to make the claim that it could be so incorporated, if of sufficient interest. So the task is to discover the status of this body of knowledge: is *it* relative? On this interpretation, 'what is to count as knowledge' means 'what is to be included in the body of received or general knowledge'.

The question seems to amount to this, can one deliberately decide, or, for that matter, inadvertently determine, what is or is not included in the body of knowledge? Can *just anything* be included or excluded? To suggest such a totally chaotic situation would be highly implausible. What is more moderately argued is rather that, since everyone who knows anything at all has a certain basic set of concepts within which, by means of which, their knowledge is expressed, if this set of concepts were changed, what in general counts as knowledge would change too. The

117

basic concepts are sometimes referred to as the 'logical framework' in existence at a given time.

It would be possible to trace quite elaborately the genesis of this idea; but roughly it seems to have arisen from a particular view of the history of science crossed with a somewhat insubstantial shadow of Strawsonian metaphysics. The most influential account, in this respect, has been that of Thomas S. Kuhn (*The Structure of Scientific Revolutions*, University of Chicago Press, 1963). Kuhn argued that between the theory of Newton and that of Einstein there was a revolution in concepts, such that one should strictly characterize some statements as *true within the context of Newtonian concepts* and others, perhaps contradictory to the first as, *true within the context of Einstein*. Similarly, it has often been said that geometrical propositions held in an unsophisticated age to be necessarily true, should properly be said to be true within the context of Euclidean geometry, there being other possible geometries. Thus there are alternative systems of physics, alternative geometries. So why could not there be an alternative history, grammar, geography, even common sense? And if there are alternatives, there is some element of choice in every statement made, however apparently necessarily true and ineluctably 'given'. If I am teaching Latin grammar it would follow that I ought to preface my explanations and examples with some such covering expression as 'Within the grammatical framework I am using' or 'In the context of *this* grammar'. Only so should I be free from the charge of imposing a choice of my own upon my pupils as though there were no choice.

However this suggestion does not really seem to merit serious consideration. For, in the first place, if absolutely every proposition we utter needs to be qualified by the preface 'within the conceptual framework we now employ' then there ceases to be any point in including the preface. Secondly, a distinction must be drawn between more and less empirical subject matter, between subject matter, that is, where the presence of theory is obtrusive and that where it is not, although such a distinction cannot be sharply drawn, or drawn for ever in one place.

Physics, at whatever level it is taught, must now be presented as a theoretical, partly abstract, study, concerned with certain explanatory hypotheses not directly subject to observation. Nature study (even if called by another name) is not to the same extent theoretical. If one is interested in, let us say, the habitat, courtship behaviour, breeding habits of the pigeon, then it is not easy to see what is meant by the suggestion that we could regard the whole subject in a totally different light. For, in contrast with physics, the relevant kinds of hypothesis (about breeding habits or habitat) are such as to be confirmed or rejected by observation of objects visible to the eyes or audible to the ears of common sense. And this is true even if sophisticated statistical methods may be used to express the observations, and justify the law-like statements based upon them, or if there is a choice of different questions to ask about pigeon life. The point of the study is to learn about the pigeons, not to learn about statistics, mathematics or probability theory, though mathematics may be used as a tool. If one is to introduce a suggestion of possible alternatives into such a study, it must be at the highly speculative level we have already considered. (We might have had a different way of distinguishing one species from another, or we might have had a different affective response to the behaviour of pigeons.) But to discuss such speculative matters is not to pursue nature study but metaphysics. There is a whole number of subjects roughly like nature study, where the same considerations apply: they are concerned more with description than with hypothesis or theory, and the descriptions are of common objects, such as we see around us every day.

Even if we confine ourselves to what are roughly speaking the more theoretical and abstract subjects, most teachers, though they introduced their remarks by the caution that what they were saying was true only relatively to a particular conceptual framework, would have little idea what an alternative framework might be. It is one thing to bow to the convention that there might be an alternative grammar, quite another to have a view as to what such a grammar (perhaps without any distinction between different tenses, moods or voices, perhaps with no distinction between nouns and verbs) might entail. It is as if I constantly referred to my husband as 'my *present* husband', which, though conveying nothing directly true or false, does suggest that divorce or remarriage are in the air. If there are no alternatives, and none are or have been considered, why put in the qualification? It can only mislead, perhaps give rise to gossip. The fact is that if you want to teach someone grammar, or history, or Euclidean geometry, you need first of all to discuss *that*, without raising questions about possible alternative concepts, different points of view or frameworks which might be employed instead of those you are employing. Of course a quite different, more philosophical, lesson could later be given on possible alternative systems. But such a lesson would be meaningless unless the pupil had *already* grasped a good deal of what was presented in the first lessons. Some knowledge of grammar, history or Euclidean geometry must be presupposed in order to make the later lesson either intelligible or interesting.

It may seem at first sight as though this entails that a teacher must either be a dishonest or an ignorant dogmatist. He must, that is to say, either know perfectly well that what he is saying is only one possible version of the facts (that the proofs he is offering do not in fact prove any proposition to be actually *true*), and pretend the opposite; or he must be too stupid and bigoted to realize that there are alternatives. In either case, it may be thought, he is misleading his pupils, though perhaps only in the first case is he actually to be blamed. But this would be a mistake. And the mistake would be of central importance, since it rests on a misconception of the very nature of knowledge. The body of knowledge which the teacher is hired to share with his pupils is in fact a body of *agreed* facts, interpretations of facts, explanations of facts, law-like statements and reductions to order of otherwise chaotic material. Where there is no agreed set of facts or interpretations, then the teacher must say so. (And of course he very commonly does. Sometimes a teacher confesses personal ignorance of what is agreed; but sometimes he tells his pupils that something or other 'is not known'.) Now it is true that, especially in the case of scientific explanations, a set of theories may be only provisional in that it may one day be superseded by another set which will explain more. But such a new set could be introduced *only* by someone who knew the old set, and could therefore understand that the old set left some phenomena unaccounted for. Thus, if science is to advance, it is essential to teach the present explanatory hypotheses with those phenomena which *are* explicable explained in terms of them. With modification, the same may be said of other, non-scientific, knowledge. But it is the essential feature of all knowledge whatever that it should be thought of as objective. It is not dependent upon any particular person, teacher or other, having asserted it, or laid claim to it, or believed it, even with conviction. It, the knowledge, is what is contained in books, articles, records and so on. Obviously no one teacher can possibly even have heard of all the knowledge that exists in this objective sense. And if all teachers died tomorrow, the books, libraries and films would enable other people, although perhaps with difficulty, to start where they had left off and add to the corpus of knowledge.

This somewhat Popper-like view of knowledge entails that knowledge is *both* objective *and* provisional (that is subject to revision). But at any point at which revision is to be introduced the necessity for it has to be shown. Some new hypothesis may indeed be introduced, but only by someone who can demonstrate that the new hypothesis explains more than the old. Thus, no one can introduce a revision who does not himself know what the old theory was, what it explained and failed to explain. A new view (a 'rewriting') of, say, biology would be of no conceivable interest, nor could it possibly make a claim to be accepted, unless introduced by someone who knew the old view and could *show* that it was lacking in explanatory power.

On such a theory of knowledge, though we may not be able to claim that what we know is truth, we may nevertheless be able to compare what is now known with what was known at an earlier stage, and claim that we are *nearer* the truth, that what we have contains *more* truth, than was available to previous students. In Popper's words, such a view 'hopefully adheres to the possibility of the growth of knowledge, and therefore of knowledge' (K. Popper, *Objective Knowledge*, OUP, 1972, p. 99). If this view of knowledge is right, then teachers have a plain duty to teach their pupils what is the received body of knowledge in their field (or at least to introduce them to it) unless they, the teachers, are themselves innovators, and may suggest to their pupils that what is received is inadequate in certain specific respects (and that teachers should be innovators is of course by no means to be ruled out, though innovators are necessarily rare, and so the situation will not often arise).

The point on which one must be clear is this: if teachers are to suggest that what is accepted as knowledge is inadequate, then they must be able to disprove it, or show it to be less adequate than an alternative. When they present their pupils with facts, they are saying 'accept this unless you can prove it wrong'. The relativist position contains some truth. The truth in it is this: it insists that one day someone may produce a revolution in all our thought about a particular subject area. And that is why it is exhilarating for pupils still at school to be introduced to the history of science, so that they may grasp that there is such a possibility. But the falsehood in relativism is that it goes on to conclude that all theories are *now* equally possible, and that none is to be preferred to any other. The possibility of revolution has blinded the relativist to the existence of a stable, received, established body of knowledge here and now. The relativist may of course long for revolution. But merely wanting to overturn received versions of science, history or geometry is not in itself sufficient to overturn them. Our first duty as teachers must be to teach what is known. And this carries with it the mark of non-relativity. One is saying 'this is how it was' or 'this is how it is'. One cannot consistently, in the same breath, say 'but it may not have been' or 'but I may be wrong'. It is nevertheless true that such statements ('this is how it is') can be seen less as claims to absolute indisputable certainty for all time, than as challenges. 'It is like this: disprove it if you can.' In practice, one must *first* show one's pupils the surrounding scene, and *then* point out that it could have been viewed from another point. The scene is still that which engages one's attention, and what must engage the attention first, before one moves on to methodological or other doubts. To adopt any other method is to attempt to allow nothing in the curriculum except philosophy. But philosophy has always been a subject to some extent parasitic on other subjects. There is no interest in a theory of knowledge without any knowledge to have a theory about.

There is therefore no reason to say that a teacher determines what shall count as knowledge in the sense in which knowledge is a common body of knowledge. And if that is so, then the question whether or not his determining it depends on his social position does not arise. Of course it is possible for teachers to be biased. But to say this is not the same as to say that there is no such thing as unbiased information, indeed it is to suggest the opposite. The unbiased is the ideal to which teachers may, more or less successfully, aspire. And to assert that a teacher may choose what to teach is not the same as to say he chooses what is true and what is false.

If there is a body of knowledge, then, it is clear that in a very broad, but very important, sense there is an educational or 'pure' criterion by which to decide what is to be included in the curriculum. Among other things, among the skills which must be included, we must include teaching part of this received corpus of knowledge. For the educated person whatever else he is, will know *more* than the uneducated, or he would not be so described. This simple view, which has had to be defended at length, excludes the view that *all* curriculum content is politically determined. For what knowledge is, is not so determined.

But whether knowledge has different forms, whether these forms dictate that there are radically different subjects, whether if so everyone ought to be taught all of these different subjects, are all of them further questions. It will be remembered that it was necessary to enter into the epistemological arguments just completed on account of the claim that the forms of knowledge, proposed as curriculum criteria by Hirst were really just a disguised defence of old-fashioned subjects, and that these were defended on political not epistemological grounds, by teachers with a vested interest in preserving them. The claim was that the concept of knowledge was itself suspect, and that if knowledge could be shown to be relative to the teacher, then teachers could have no right to claim the sanctity of 'subjects', their particular preferred corner of alleged knowledge. Instead, an "open" curriculum should be created, in which pupils and teachers together determined what was to be explored in any given class. Specialist accumulation of "facts" would be at an end. The short statement of such a view is that if there is no such thing as knowledge, *a fortiori* it cannot be the passing on of knowledge which determines the content of the curriculum (with the corollary that people have clung to the pretence of knowledge as a means of power). We are now in a position where we can deny the premiss and assert boldly that knowledge exists. So there are good grounds for falling back on the common-sense view. No reason has been found why we should *not* say that curriculum content is a matter of knowledge to be passed on. But from this nothing follows with respect to the ways in which knowledge should be divided up. What we have done is answer the radical objection that knowledge is a myth. But we have done nothing to settle the less radical question of how to select or organize what knowledge to teach.

The theory that there is a specific number of totally different forms of knowledge was, however, seen to be unproved. Moreover Hirst did not even claim to *prove* that everyone ought to have some knowledge in all its different forms. He just asserted that it was so. Now one of the objections to the kind of curriculum which would be based on Hirst's theory was that it would tend to get both teachers and pupils involved in meta-subjects, in defining historical thinking rather than learning history, in showing that a course on the life cycle of the dragon-fly was a specimen or example of scientific thinking in general; in ensuring that while reading Shakespeare you realized that what you were doing was appreciating and criticizing Great Literature at large. This objection is serious. For it might lead in practice to a kind of disengagement from the field to be studied not unlike that generated, as we saw, by the relativist theory of knowledge itself. There we were in danger of learning only about the possibility of alternative conceptual frameworks; here we are in danger of learning only the way in which one form of knowledge differs from another. But if there is indeed a body of knowledge to be learned, it seems more important that pupils should have a chance to learn some part of it first and then, if they want to, reflect on what learning it was like (as well perhaps, as on whether it could all have been different). It is interesting, no doubt, to those of a speculative turn of mind to raise the question what is the difference between historical and scientific evidence. But such speculations should follow, if at all, on learning about actual courses of events, and actual scientific conclusions. Just so it may well be of absorbing interest to some to envisage an alternative to Einstein. But that should come after learning about the magnet or the nature of sound waves. It is important, that is, not to distance people too far from what they are to know. The time may come when it is necessary to say, with the *New Yorker*, 'Just give the facts, please.'

In general, the question how knowledge is to be divided up for pedagogical purposes can be seen to be far less important than the question whether there is any knowledge to be divided up at all. Once we are satisfied that there *is* knowledge, and that the teacher's task is to teach it, then the considerations which should weigh with the curriculum designer may well turn out to be relatively practical. First, and obviously, children must be taught the skills which will enable them to acquire knowledge for themselves; and this means not only reading and writing, but knowledge of how to frame questions, how to look things up, how to criticize what other people tell them. Apart from this, what knowledge teachers are to share with or impart to their pupils will be determined according to what will be interesting, useful, fruitful of further knowledge, and perhaps by other tests. If subject barriers should be crossed it will be because one traditional subject illumines another, or because the advance of knowledge has brought to light new connexions, making the traditional subject classifications out of date. Some subjects are more suitable to be taught at school than others because they are more basic, some because they have a universal appeal.

Given that there is a whole range of different criteria by which to choose items of the curriculum, there will necessarily always be a certain tension, competing claims for inclusion. This seems to be not only inevitable but actually desirable, if the school curriculum is not to become a wholly fixed immutable scheme, exactly embodying a particular theory of knowledge, as the curriculum proposed by Plato was. Moreover, since it is impossible that everyone should learn everything, there will have to remain an element of choice in the curriculum. If knowledge is to be pursued at least partly on the grounds that it is interesting then allowance must be made for the fact that people's interests are different. Thus what is to be taught in any educational curriculum will, on this view, always remain a matter for negotiation, for an attempt at agreement on the part of the curriculum builders as to what is important, what interesting, what positively indispensable. But all the argument in defence of particular items for inclusion will be educational, in the sense that they will take the form 'One is better educated if one knows this than if one does not', an unexciting, even circular, form of argument, but impossible to replace by any other.

There is a further crucial point which may be of some help to us. If there is knowledge, but if we are trying to find ways of selecting knowledge to pass on, one criterion of selection will be the future of the pupil. Education in the sense which is the whole subject of this book comes to an end at some stage: it is not the goal of life; it leads to something else. That a curriculum is determined according to educational criteria does not entail that those who design it should have no regard to what is to happen next. On the contrary, if education is not the whole of life, educational criteria will necessarily be forward-looking. A curriculum designer must consider what lies behind the curriculum. To be educationally defensible means, in part, to be what will improve life *as a whole*. Knowledge and skills are both taught with an eye to the future. This is so obvious a point that it might seem hardly worth making. But very often those who would defend 'purely' educational, as opposed to 'political' criteria for the design of a curriculum speak as though to be 'pure', knowledge must be pursued for its own sake, and not pursued because it will be needed by the pupil in his life outside the classroom. Sometimes, for example, those who defend the educational, distinguish sharply between 'education' on the one hand and 'socialization' on the other. We may consider again Michael Oakeshott's essay 'Education: the Engagement and its Frustration' (*Op. cit.*, see page 12). There he argues that education proper begins 'with the appearance of a teacher with something to impart which is *not* immediately connected with the current wants or interests of the learner', and again, 'School is a place apart, in which the heir may encounter his moral and intellectual inheritance not in the terms in which it is being used in the current engagements and occupations of the world outside . . . but as an estate, entire unqualified and unencumbered'. Yet more explicitly another defender of the pure, John Wilson, writes 'So long as we are concerned to turn out pupils who are good middle class boys or skilled technicians' then we are not really concerned with education but with *training*. 'For whereas we can train and adapt pupils for particular roles and performances, what we have to educate is people.' The suggestion is clear. On some definition or other of 'a person' (about which Wilson tells us we ought to 'get clear') we can discover what educating a person will consist in; but whatever it consists in, it will not be directly related to the roles and tasks which that person will be called on to fulfil after his education is over ('Integration of the Maladjusted' in *The Integration of Handicapped Children in Society*, edited by J. Loring and G. Barnn, Routledge and Kegan Paul, 1972).

It is to be noticed that those who wish to draw some distinction like Oakeshott's or John Wilson's often have recourse to emotive expressions such as to 'turn out', with their strong suggestion of the school as factory, the classroom as assembly line. But such phrases apart, the distinction they make is one which common sense, on the whole, rejects. Apart from dubious distinctions between pupils and persons, the question is whether we want to distinguish knowledge from useful knowledge, or people from people-fulfilling-a-role. Common sense at any rate inclines to think of education as a preparation for life; and of life as better if the people living it have roles to fill, useful things to do.

So, if education would be agreed to be pointless if it did not lead to, or contribute to, a better life for those who received it, then, having established that the contents of the curriculum should be determined in accordance with educational criteria, we have finally to consider what is and what is not a better life. For the two notions (that of education and the good life) cannot be separated.

IV

The Good Life

So we have arrived at the final unavoidable question, what are the ingredients of the good life, in pursuit of which we undertake to educate people? How are we to tell whether the education on offer is successful or not? How are we to judge whether other things being equal, people's lives will be better after they have received it? Without some standard of judgement, there can be no standard by which to determine what should and what should not form part of the educational curriculum.

When faced with so vast a subject matter, it is necessary to chart a course in some way; and my discussion will fall into three parts. My three headings are Virtue, Work, and Imagination.

(a) VIRTUE

Aristotle says about pleasure and happiness, that there must be some connexion between them, because no one would really conceive of happiness who did not weave the notion of pleasure somehow into his ideal. Similarly, the notion of morality must be in some way connected with that of the good life, though they are not identical. It is certain at any rate that there is a general hope, for those who go to school, that they may be taught to be morally good, among other things that they are taught. And in so far as schools aim to educate their pupils, they also take some responsibility for moral education.

Part of the reason for this is that it is children who go to school; and children whether at home or at school are in need

E   129

of being taught how to behave, how to be morally good. For children, as J. S. Mill said, are not naturally moral. They may be naturally affectionate, but nevertheless they need to learn to modify their selfishness and even their affections, and this is the essence of morality. They spend a great deal of time at school, in constant contact with other people, and so it will necessarily be there that they learn a great part of their duties, responsibilities and powers with regard to other people. School, moreover, will probably provide their first all-important contact with a world which does not consist of their own family, a world of which they are not the centre, and which does not consist of people especially committed to *them*. They take their place among others equally important. For these reasons a school is, and must be, a school of morals, and a good school will teach its pupils to behave well. But to say this is far from saying that in any formal sense morality should be part of the curriculum. What is sometimes referred to as 'the hidden curriculum' may be more important than the overt in this area of teaching. We must proceed to consider whether this is so or not.

A great deal has been written recently about moral education and how morality should be taught. It is perhaps possible, without too much distortion, to pick out a general tendency in this literature. In moral philosophy, there has grown up a tradition, in the main accepted by educationalists, that morality is primarily a matter of making decisions. Moral choice, the moment when one has to decide whether or not to do the tempting thing, the dilemma in which either of two alternatives seems to carry bad consequences, these are taken to be the central dramas of morality, with reference to which the nature of morality must be elucidated. Historically, this tradition stems from the Kantian notion that it is in moral choices alone that human beings exercise freedom. From Kant also, in part, derives the idea that such choices, to be both moral and free, must be rational, and rational in a particular way. The writings of R. M. Hare have reinforced this tradition (especially *Freedom and Reason*, Oxford, 1963). According to Hare, morality is a matter of a particular *form of judgement* which is fundamentally imperative in mood. To be a morally good person, one must from time to time utter commands to oneself which one would be prepared to conceive as commands to other people as well, and which one could justify by showing how they arise from a first principle, itself a command. Thus rationally deriving a particular command from a general principle is at the centre of morality, and to teach morality must be to teach this kind of process. It is a process which ends with a decision, expressed in the formula 'do this!'

Such a view of the teaching of morals is sometimes expressed in the language of Paul Hirst: morality is a particular and distinguishable form of knowledge, or form of thought. The knowledge in question is knowledge of how to make rational and defensible decisions. A characteristic version of the theory is to be found in a paper entitled 'Moral Education and the Curriculum by John Wilson (in *Progress and Problems in Moral Education*, edited by Monica Taylor, National Foundation for Educational Research, 1975), and it is worth examining his arguments a little further. He advocates quite specifically that, at school, one or two periods a week should be devoted to the teaching of morality, and he urges the publication of coherent material for teachers to use in the lessons. This material would list, in handy form, the concepts, procedures, types of reasons and abilities which are basic to the subject of morality, 'explaining what is required for moral thought and action in a quite straightforward and workmanlike manner' (*Op. cit.*, p. 38). Such a handbook, he claims, would not be a book of philosophy, still less of morality, but of *methodology*. The aim of the material would not be to introduce particular controversial issues for discussion, as is often done in schools, but, perhaps with the help of very simple examples, to stress the point that 'there are right and wrong, rational and irrational, serious and non-serious ways of making up one's mind on moral issues'. The argument is that morality has its own methodology and principles, and these should be taught separately, just as the principles and methods of arithmetic should. Only so, when real moral issues crop up and decisions have to be taken, can one hope that pupils will settle them properly. Elsewhere (in *A Teacher's Guide to Moral Education*, Chapman, 1973), Wilson suggested that the principles in question will lay down a kind of rational utilitarianism, whose aim is to ensure that, in moral decisions, everyone should count for one and none for more than one.

Despite Wilson's disclaimers, it is obvious that such rationalism is in fact a particular theory of morality. It represents one powerful school of moral philosophy. As such it may interest the pupils, even influence their ways of thought, but it cannot teach them to *be moral*, that is to behave well, and it was this, as part of the function of school, that we began by talking about. For in real life morality is exceedingly unlike arithmetic. In practising the kind of reasoning appropriate to arithmetic and in using examples (such as calculating the speed of a specific train, or working out how long it would take to empty a bath with a pipe of a certain dimension) one is in a sense actually doing arithmetic. Mathematics is an abstract subject, and one can therefore do it in the classroom, although it may be outside the classroom that it will have its practical application. But morality has not got this abstract life of its own. There is therefore no sense to be attached to saying one can 'do' it in the classroom, and apply it later, as need arises. There is no such thing as 'doing morality', only behaving well or badly, and behaviour needs real contexts, not merely exemplary ones.

Moreover, behaving well, though it doubtless includes the reaching of good decisions at particular times and on specific occasions, does not consist in this alone. For we may hold that even a good decision needs something else before it can certainly be properly so described. It needs, in Aristotle's words, to arise out of a 'steady and unalterable state of character'. It is not just rationality which needs to be shown in moral decisions; they must also be manifestations of virtue. It may even be that the more a man has a fixed and steady disposition the less he has to take decisions at all. He may behave well, that is truthfully, loyally, bravely, kindly, fairly, without being much tempted by the opposite course. It may scarcely occur to him as a possibility. Yet we could not deny that he was a morally good man. Teaching a certain kind of argument would hardly go any way at all towards teaching someone to be of this kind. Casuistry may be great fun, but character-training, odious though it sounds, may be more what people hope for when they first send their children to school.

Wilson anticipates objections to his scheme. But so convinced is he of its unique correctness that he prefers not to call them objections but 'resistances' (that well-known psycho-analytic term, designed to make you feel terrible for refusing to accept as true something either false or meaningless). We resist, according to Wilson, because the programme he proposes is threatening. The resisters say (as I have just said) that morality is not a matter of learning to argue, and that teaching it is a question of 'example or inspiration or cold baths and rugger or tea and sympathy or whatever' (p. 36). But they say this, Wilson alleges, because the programme proposed is 'too much like hard work'. It is, he concludes, 'easier to act out our fantasies'. Later (p. 45) he returns to the expected forms of resistance to his theory (and here the word 'prejudice' is used as an alternative to 'resistance'). Potential teachers and pupils may, he suggests, think 'in a different mode' from that which he holds to be correct. Instead of calculating other people's interests alongside their own, they may, he says, think in the mode of obeying some external authority (such as the law, for example); or in the 'self obeying' mode, in which some internal feeling on the part of the pupil determines what he ought to do. 'This may be guilt or shame ("conscience") or perhaps some ideal of himself that he is wedded to.' Presumably persons who think in this second 'mode' may either not believe that morality is a matter of making rational decisions, or, more plausibly, may believe that there is more to morality than this alone. Now doubtless it is true that if morality were as Wilson suggests, then it could be taught in the way he proposes. And if this were the case, he would be right to deny the relevance both of example or inspiration, as methods of teaching, and of having an ideal of oneself, or experiencing shame, as an element in practical morality. For no one would suggest teaching arithmetic by inducing the pupil to contemplate the example of good practitioners, nor would they suggest that thinking of oneself as a mathematician would cause one to become good at arithmetic (though it might in fact help quite a lot). But the truth is that Wilson has underestimated the complexity of morality. For though there is no doubt that consideration of the interests of others is a central part of morality, and indeed that there would be no morality without it, it is also true, and not at all incompatible, that to be moral one *must*, to a large extent, 'act out one's fantasies'. The difference, obviously, between the good and the bad lies in what fantasies they each have.

Everyone agrees that bad actions are often committed as part of a fantasy (the vision of oneself as tough, for instance, or as irresistible to the opposite sex). It is also true that many, but not all, good actions have the same source. One may see oneself as having a certain standard of honesty or generosity, for instance, and refrain from acts of dishonesty, meanness or jealousy which, in conflicting with this picture, would cause shame. What else is pursuing an ideal? The notion that the pursuit of an ideal can have nothing to do with morality is an absurd narrowing of the concept. Of course we want children to be rational. But we also want them to be truthful, hardworking, understanding, generous and virtuous in other ways. Why is only rationality to be taught? It is tempting to answer that it is because rationality can more easily be taught in two periods a week as a school subject (though that is doubtful). But that would be to accuse Wilson of using a circular argument.

In any case, employing a particular kind of reasoning and becoming adept at it will not guarantee that even the utilitarian pleasure/pain calculus will be worked out when the real time for decision-making comes. Wilson suggests that children should be taught how to argue with regard to the interest of others, and this is very good. But teaching methodology will not ensure that they actually *want* other people's interests to be looked after as well as their own. To want this genuinely is to have a certain kind of character or disposition. It is not prejudice or mere irrational 'resistance' to say that what we want for our

134

children, as much as for ourselves, is that they and we should have certain qualities of character. We judge what is good and we admire, all at once. And if someone behaves well and we admire him, if for instance he is conspicuously honest, or if he goes out of his way to help someone with no expectation of reward, we do not withdraw our admiration on the grounds that he did not decide what to do according to the correct methods of reasoning. Nor do we wait to admire until we ourselves have argued our way into that frame of mind, or at least we need not do so. A man does not have to prove to us that he has acted well. We can learn that he has, from experience.

If this learning by experience is an important part of learning what it is to be morally good, as I would maintain, then it follows that this part of morality must be taught to children by example. This is a harsh doctrine, but one accepted it seems to me, implicitly, by all those teachers we would regard as good, in any kind of school. For the virtues which a good teacher has to exercise in the classroom may seem trivial, because they are confined within the boundaries of a particular, unexciting, context, and are an everyday part of a childish experience. But they are the very same virtues which are not trivial when exercised within a wider sphere; and they can be seen to be non-trivial by pupils as they get older. A teacher can be fair or unfair, honest or dishonest (pretending to knowledge he hasn't got, for instance), kind or cruel, forgiving or relentless, generous or mean. If he himself exercises these virtues then he is also in a position to reproach his pupils for failing to do so, and if they like what they see in him, they will begin to dislike the opposite in themselves. All this is part of the everyday currency of school conversation. Everybody knows that children, and pupils at school who are not children, admire some virtues in their teachers, and despise some vices. It is far easier for children to see the qualities of character possessed by their teachers as good or bad than it is for them to make similar judgements about their parents. It is therefore all the more necessary for teachers to know what they are at, what characteristics they are displaying, since their virtues and vices will form a part of the whole picture of possible moral behaviour that a child will, gradually, build up.

The danger of teaching morals ('doing morality') in the manner recommended by Wilson is that it would tend to put the subject into a separate compartment and trivialize it. Here, if anywhere, there seems to be a powerful argument against 'subject barriers'. We all know that it is difficult to relate classroom French to the living language spoken in France, or to connect 'school' literature with what one might want to read on one's own account. It seems an unnecessary hazard to introduce a situation in which, having done one's morals prep. for the week, one can forget it. To discuss moral issues, current controversies is one thing. This may be a part both of clarifying one's ideas and of keeping informed about what is going on. Even moral philosophy might have a place in the curriculum if there were some enthusiastic teacher who could make it interesting. But this, as Wilson himself insists, is not what he means by the teaching of morals. But we must conclude that he has not made a case for the kind of 'workmanlike' exposition which he advocates.

There are a few further, related, points to be made in connexion with the teaching of virtue. The first can be dealt with quite briefly. It is the question of rules. There are two distinct ways in which it is customary to introduce the notion of rules into educational discussions. First, it is sometimes suggested (see, for instance, R. S. Peters, *Ethics and Education*, Allen and Unwin, 1966) that teachers must teach their pupils the *basic moral rules* without which society would be impossible, and that these rules will govern life at school as well as in the world at large. 'Rules like those prohibiting injury to the person, theft, lying, and the breaking of contracts are necessary for the life of a school as well as for that of any other community. Any teacher must insist on the observance of such rules both from the point of view of the maintenance of necessary conditions of order in the school and from the point of view of moral education.' So Peters writes (*op. cit.*, p. 173). But it seems to me that it is a source of confusion of a somewhat damaging kind to speak in this context of *rules*. If one considers what are generally called rules at school it will be obvious that these are specific regulations with regard to such things as the marking of clothes, the production of explanatory notes in case of absence, the seeking of permission to leave the school grounds during the day and other such matters. For all these rules there is probably a good reason and that reason can be given if required. The rules, moreover, having been made, perhaps over a period of time, could be changed, uniform might be abandoned, the rule prohibiting the wearing of stiletto heels might be removed from the list because of a change in fashion and so on.

It is undesirable to include in the list of school rules anything that is not specific, or which does not relate exclusively to persons who are in the school. The school rules, that is, regulate behaviour in a quite explicitly narrow field, with reference only to pupils in the school as long as they are in the school. This is an absolutely typical and central function of a set of rules. On the whole, the justification of the rules will be convenience, safety, orderliness and other such non-moral considerations. Again, though certain items in the list of rules may be questioned or changed from time to time, as long as an item is included, one can demand obedience to it simply on the ground that it is a rule. Rules, then, are useful partly because, though the presence of a rule in the list could usually be justified, yet they need not be justified every time they are applied. Moreover conformity to the rule is *all* that is required. It does not matter whether people are willing or unwilling, whole- or half-hearted in their conformity to the rule about absence notes. All that matters is that the absence note be produced. Often the rules prohibit behaviour, such as running in the corridors or wearing red socks, which, apart from the fact that it is prohibited by the rules for the pupils in school, is perfectly acceptable.

So-called moral rules are utterly different in all these respects. For instance, in the case of morals, what is wanted is essentially a certain attitude, specifically an attitude towards other people. The teacher hopes, for example, that his pupils will not tease a newcomer, or persecute a fellow pupil because he is black or too small or a supporter of the wrong football team; but he does not hope that they will refrain from such behaviour in obedience to a rule, but out of sympathy and consideration. A rule against bullying or theft would be an absurdity. It would suggest that the school had made the rule for some reason of convenience, and that, apart from the existence of the rule, there might be nothing against bullying or theft, or that it made no difference from what motive one refrains from them. In very rare circumstances, perhaps when one thought one's pupils too young or too stupid to understand a moral point, one might invent a 'moral rule'. But the sooner such a rule could be dispensed with the better. A teacher would have failed in his duty if all he had succeeded in passing on to his pupils was that certain forms of behaviour were 'ruled out'.

It seems to me of the greatest importance in the teaching of morality at school to distinguish between those forms of behaviour which are immoral (perhaps, but not necessarily, contrary to a moral *principle*) and those which are simply against the rules. One can insist that neither form of behaviour be practised, but the supporting arguments in each case will be utterly different. To fail to draw such a distinction is actually to fail to teach morality, which is essentially a matter of wanting to be of a certain kind, of wanting not to fall below a certain standard in one's dealings with others.

If a teacher adopted Peters's suggestion and taught some 'moral rules', he would presumably state these *as* rules, which existed, but had not been made by anyone. The second way in which the notion of a rule is brought to bear on the teaching in school is different from this and more obscure. I mention it only in case it should be confused with the previous use. In the relatively new field of educational sociology, any regularity of behaviour tends to be described by reference to a rule. Behaviour which is eccentric or different from the normal is then called 'deviant' (and questions may then be raised about, for instance, what effect it has on a pupil to be picked out as deviant by his teacher). Such a vocabulary is employed in an attempt to adopt a quasi-anthropological approach to the analysis of school

The Good Life

life. This use of the term 'rule' is analogous in some respects to that found in linguistics, or in the philosophy of language (where philosophers sometimes say that to learn the meaning of a word is to learn the 'rules for its use'). The suggestion in this use of the term is that there may be rules governing behaviour which can be detected as rules by an outside observer, but which are not recognized as rules by those who act either in accordance with them or deviantly. In this sense, rules are rather like agreed conventions, which may be accepted in society but never made explicit. Breach of such conventions (such as those governing kinds of dress or habits of greeting people in the street) may be regarded as eccentric (unconventional) but not normally as *wrong*; and certainly conventions are distinct from principles. It seems to me that the use of the word 'rule' to cover such cases is confusing. It combines the senses of 'regularity' and 'regulation', and muddles the issue of whether or not anybody laid down the rule, and whether anyone, except the observer, would agree that there was a rule. For all these reasons it seems to spread darkness rather than light.

However, this is really a digression. Let us return to the 'moral rules' of Peters's formulation (which I have argued are not properly rules at all). One of the arguments he gives in favour of the teaching of such a specific and limited code is that it defines an area of moral teaching which a teacher must pass on to his pupils as objective and universally valid. If the teacher strays beyond what is included in the code, it is his duty to label what he says as his *opinion*. With regard to such views, Peters says (*Op. cit.*, p. 202) 'the teacher has no right to use the special relationship in which he stands to children to parade his own idiosyncratic opinions. . . . His concern should not be to convert children to adopt such substantive positions . . . but to get them to see the reasons on which such positions are based; for his job is teaching not indoctrination.' Since these bold words were written a great deal more has been said about the distinction between teaching and indoctrination, and about the need for a teacher to remain neutral, and allow his pupils to make up their own minds on all controversial matters. We have seen

139

already how pervasive is the fear, in much current educational theory, of a teacher's passing on his bias to his pupils in the matter of 'what should count as knowledge'. In the field of morals the fear is stronger still, in proportion as the view that the whole thing is subjective, 'a matter of opinion', is more widely held.

The arguments in favour of moral commitment on the teacher's part (by this I mean his attempting to teach his pupils to be good and virtuous, according to his moral standards) are in some ways parallel to those in favour of his teaching his share of the body of knowledge, uninhibited by protestations of the relativity of all knowledge. For I have argued so far in this chapter that the teacher must open the eyes of his pupils to what morality is, to what it is to want to be moral by manifestly wanting to be so himself. He must plainly show that he cares about such virtues as honesty and sympathy. He cannot do this, if at the same time he has to suggest that his caring about honesty is just a matter of opinion, of taste, perhaps. As a matter of fact, even in cases which might more readily be agreed to be matters of taste, no teacher would *simply* say 'I like this, you need not' and leave it at that. He would at least try to show to his pupils what was likeable about the object in question; and if he very much liked and enjoyed the object, his doing so would shine through his exposition and give it a force it would not otherwise have. And no one would blame him for this. If this is so in aesthetic matters, with regard to which we are more prepared to to say 'you can take it or leave it alone', it is still more so with regard to morals.

The point is this: you cannot teach morality without being committed to morality yourself; and you cannot be committed to morality yourself without holding that some things are right and others wrong. You cannot hold that, and at the same time sincerely maintain that someone else's view of the matter may be equally good. Of course, as everyone has always known (both philosophers and real people) there are different views about what is right and what wrong. We can admit that there were people who held that it was all right, even right, to expose weakly infants or torture those who held different religious beliefs. But that some people have differed from us need not make us change our views, or suppose that we may be wrong. It is easy, admittedly, to say this with regard to alternative moralities which are either defunct, or very far distant in space, less easy if we come upon vast differences here and now. But the principle is the same. If members of the IRA believe sincerely that they are justified in planting bombs without warning, in undergrounds or in pubs, then we must be prepared to condemn them, if we think they are wrong. Children will learn soon enough that there is more than one view of the rights and wants of other people. What we want is that they should be resolute in defending their own moral position. They will not learn to do this if they have never experienced anyone who *does* whole-heartedly defend what he believes to be right.

Of course the teacher will have a duty to ensure that the grounds on which he bases his moral judgement are good, that the facts he alleges are, as far as he can discover, true. But he will be failing in his duty if, having presented the facts, he refuses to draw any moral conclusion from them. After all, I have argued that much of his teaching is to be practical, in the playground, and in the classroom, and in the dinner queue, indifferently. His teaching may arise in the context of any aspect of life, not just in the Morals lesson. So, very often, his judgement will *have* to be of a practical kind. 'You did wrong to pretend to have read what you haven't read. Read it now.' 'You did wrong to take the tennis racquet which you knew wasn't yours. Give it back.' Young children, at least, need action; and I suppose that everyone would agree that in such cases the teacher has no duty to remain neutral (though he must be impartial). Nor need he preface his remarks by saying 'according to the morality of our culture' or some other such modest subjectivizing phrase.

But if this is true, why should he remain neutral in discussion? Why should it be supposed that older children, too, do not learn from clear and decisive moral views being avowed and even implemented in practice? If the teacher is a moral agent he must have views, principles, attitudes, even passions. And it is only if he is seen to be a moral agent that he can teach his pupils to be moral agents too.

The famous Socratic question was 'Can virtue be taught?' Socrates assumed that it would be desirable, if possible. We, more nervous, need first to raise the question do we want it to be taught? I have suggested in the earlier part of the chapter that we do. But if we want it taught, can it be? Again I suggest that the answer is yes, but not in special lessons, nor, it now seems, by a teacher claiming neutrality as between different claimants to *be* virtue. A teacher must be brave enough to try to share his picture of the virtuous person with his pupils. Of course a child or an adolescent can learn by example only if the example is of the *sincere* preference for the good over the bad, the nice over the nasty. And this constitutes another argument against having special morals classes. For in the morals lessons there will presumably be only discussion, not much action. And if within the allotted forty minutes the teacher does express admiration or scorn, if he, in short, expresses, even sincerely, his moral beliefs, there will still remain the suspicion that he is doing so to order, for the purpose of setting a good example, and so his teaching will come to nothing. Gilbert Ryle put the matter thus: '... in matters of morality as distinct from techniques, good examples had better not be set with an edifying purpose. For such a would-be improving exhibition of, say, indignation, would be an insincere exhibition; the vehemence of the denunciation would be a parent's, a pedagogue's or a pastor's histrionics. The example authentically set would be that of edifyingly shamming indignation. So it would be less hazardous to reword Socrates's original question and ask not "can virtue be taught?" but "can virtue be learned?".' He goes on to argue that learning by example is to be distinguished from mere aping, and from conditioning. 'It is certainly true that without conditioning the child will acquire neither conversational English nor manners nor morals nor a Yorkshire accent. But aping does not suffice to get the child to the higher stage of making and following new remarks in English, of behaving politely in a new situation, or of making allowance in a competitive game for a handicapped newcomer. He now has to *think* like his elder brother or the hero of his adventure story, i.e. to think for himself. He now has to emulate their non-echoings.' (Gilbert Ryle, 'Can Virtue be Taught?' in *Education and the Development of Reason*, edited by Dearden, Hirst and Peters, Routledge and Kegan Paul, 1972.)

So far, in the attempt to discover what should be in the curriculum as contributing to the good life, we have reached the somewhat negative conclusion that morality should not be in the curriculum. But nevertheless something has been gained. For we have at least concluded that morality, or virtuousness, should be taught, and can be learned, though not in special lessons. However this leaves us with, as it were, an empty time-table. We must still try to find out on what criterion to admit things to fill the spaces.

(b) WORK

It is agreed so far that what is to fill the timetable is what will contribute to the good life. I now want to put forward a candidate for inclusion which satisfies that criterion. I will argue that children should learn at school what will help them to work for the rest of their lives. A number of objections to this view can be raised. Before considering them, it must be made clear that the goal of work is only one of the goals which education should have; there are others (at least one other). This is an important point, since it is sometimes said that if education is directed solely towards work, then those who are unemployable for any reason, such as disability or old age, will be miserable; and that those who are known never to be employable will seem not to merit education. According to this argument one ought to educate at least as much for leisure as for work, or perhaps not specifically *for* either. Again, it is argued that in periods of high unemployment, or in a future more highly automated age, work may be necessarily sporadic, and have to be seen as the exception in a person's life. If so, work should not be the goal of education. Finally, it is argued that education for work is too narrow and 'vocational' to be desirable. But, while conceding a certain point to these objections, as I hope will become clear later, I would nevertheless maintain that work is, and must always be an important ingredient in the good life; that a life without work would always be less good than a life which contained it; and that to be totally unemployed is indeed a dreadful fate. One should help people, no doubt, to bear it, but should not accept it as a normal or ultimately tolerable condition.

I have laid down with apparent dogmatism that work is part of a good life. But notoriously work varies in the degree of satisfaction it offers. Schemes for job-enlargement, job-enrichment, the involvement of workers in decision-making at various levels are all of them concerned with increasing satisfaction in work, even if they are also concerned with increasing output and efficiency, as side-effects. Such schemes emphasize the extent to which work may be boring, or may seem pointless to those who undertake it. To be alienated from one's work is to regard it as *simply* a way of earning money, necessary and probably evil. I am not here concerned with the degree to which routine or nasty jobs could be made better. I want to maintain that even where a job is bad in all kinds of ways, it is better to have it than not, and probably better to work hard at it than less hard. It is certainly true (and in periods of high unemployment likely to be generally recognized) that money earned is better than money handed out as a right, divorced from any work done. The vast distinction between pocket money and the same amount of money first earned, perhaps from a newspaper round, is a distinction never entirely lost sight of. Nor is this mere sentimentality. For it is in the nature of a hand-out or gift that the receiver is in an inferior position. Not only is it more blessed, it is well known to be in other ways nicer to give than to receive. It is hard to reconcile oneself to being the object of charity. Pride, self-esteem, confidence in one's own powers are all outraged by receiving money in exchange for nothing, even if one does regard the money as, in some sense, one's legal right. So to this extent any work is better than none, if it is paid, and this is not in conflict with the obvious truth that some forms of work are more satisfactory than others.

Not all work of course is, or could ever be, paid. But even unpaid work, just in so far as it is work and could properly be so described, is something which has value for the person who goes in for it. There is a kind of convention that people should present themselves as fundamentally hostile to work. They do not wish to be thought of as subscribing to the puritanical or bourgeois work-ethic. And so hardly anyone avows a preference for work over idleness. If one says 'it must have been hard work', whether one is referring to setting up a new company, learning a new concerto or digging a new garden, one tends to say it in a tone of solicitude, even commiseration. But extraordinarily often people will admit that it was hard work, but fun or enjoyable. And even more often, surveying their lives as a whole, they are prepared to concede that the periods of hard work were the best, even that, on the whole, they have preferred work to holidays, and certainly would not have cared for holidays if there had not been long compensating spells of work. So merely doing something which could be called work, though it may be something we have to pretend to wish to avoid, and quite genuinely be something we have to steel ourselves to begin, seems in fact to be something we value for its own sake, as well as for its reward. I suspect that Nietzsche, at least, would not be at all surprised at this. For he would argue that all human motives are compounded of various desires to control, to manipulate, to use, in other words to dominate the environment. Indeed in his view all causation in the non-conscious world, as well as all motivation in the human world, is a matter of the same 'will'. The will to power in this large sense is perhaps identical with the will to work. After all, even organizing a strike is only changing one kind of work for another, perhaps more congenial, kind. It is certain that all work is effort to make or change things or reduce them to order, and that all these efforts are worth making. We value them, because we want to be in control of things, on however small a scale; and it is a source of satisfaction to be so. For to be able to control or adapt things is to exercise our freedom. Work is therefore a proof of human freedom. At a less portentous level, too, one is, to a certain extent, free in proportion to one's capacity to work. On a desert island, the more one could work to produce what was needed for life, the more free one would be. In the non-desert-island situation we most of us occupy, one is free in proportion as one can *sell* one's work. The desire to work and to earn is therefore obviously part of the desire to be free. (Receiving charity is, in this sense, the opposite of freedom.)

These general truths, however obvious, have to be stated, because it is with them as background that the notion of educating for work has to be justified. For, as we saw at the end of Chapter III, there is a considerable body of opinion hostile to the idea that one should teach children at school with an eye to what they will do, how they will work, when they leave school. It is felt on the one hand that this may suggest a return to the concept of educating the working classes and other classes differently; of giving to the working classes the modest training in the way of reading, writing and arithmetic that they will actually use at work, and giving them nothing else. On the other hand it is also supposed that looking beyond school (or university) to what is going to be needed afterwards, will lead to the end of academic freedom at a higher level of education.

As to this second point, one must be careful to distinguish two elements here. First, if children are to be educated in such a way that they can get jobs, it is reasonable that someone must try to work out roughly what kinds of jobs there will be for them. Detailed planning with regard to the numbers of doctors, engineers and so on to be educated for the future has been notoriously misleading and unreliable. But all the same, planning, however bad its name, must be expected to go on. It is not outrageous for a government, which directly or indirectly finances most education, including university education, to attempt to ensure that there is a rational justification, for instance, for opening a new medical or law school, or for spending money on educating people as foresters or pharmacists. So in advising pupils what to do, teachers are bound to take account of the numbers of vacancies in higher education and employment in any particular field. But, secondly, this kind of central control is very different from control over the actual content of the syllabus to be taught. If government began literally to control what was taught, then indeed academic freedom would be at an end; and it is the fear that the first kind of control will inevitably lead to the second that causes people to adopt extreme positions like those of Oakeshott and John Wilson, cited in the last chapter. But, as so often, these fears are exaggerated, and lead to an exaggerated reaction.

To return now to the first point, if it is true that people actually *want* to work, then it would be a disservice to them to educate them in such a way that this desire was less likely to be satisfied. But this does not entail that, right from the start of a child's life at school, he should be destined for a *certain sort* of work. There is such a thing as social mobility; a child whose father is a panel-basher may not wish to have that, or any comparable job. And if he starts on the factory floor he may end as a director. We must not cut down on anybody's education as if we were a caste society. To say this is not to deny that there are social classes, but only to say that their barriers are capable of being breached, and that education is, for any individual, a good way to breach them, though by no means the only way. It must always remain true that some professions demand more education over a longer period of time than others. The ideal of a curriculum should be that what everyone begins with should be useful for the next step, so that at the stage where some people leave school they will be qualified for work, while those who stay will be qualified for the next bit of education. This is admittedly a difficult ideal, perhaps impossible to attain, since what is a sensible thing to do if you are next going to learn a new subject, say economics or psychology or archaeology, may not be a sensible thing to do if you are next going to be an apprentice carpenter, or learn to be a waiter. Nevertheless a common framework for the curriculum at school up to the earliest age at which pupils may leave is not difficult to conceive. The crucial point, as will I hope become clear later, is that within the framework there should be enough diversity to accommodate different interests. Ideally also it ought to be possible to go back, if not to school, then at least to a grown-up equivalent of school, and pick up where you left off, so that it should be easy to spend two years, even much more, being a waiter, and then decide after all to aim to become a solicitor or a journalist.

How are schools to tell what it is that will help a child to satisfy his desire to work? This is not really very difficult. Schools must to a certain extent sink their scruples and consent to listen to what it is that the outside world demands. If industry wants people who can calculate and understand complicated plans and read a balance sheet, then industry must say so and pupils must be taught. There is nothing ideologically harmful in this. If the universities want a certain competence in, say, reading and understanding both English and other languages, and the ability to write clearly, then this must be taught. It is absurd to suppose that no account should be taken at school of what will count as a qualification for the next stage: people do not stay at school for ever. To know that arithmetic will be useful to you later does not mysteriously reduce the value of learning it, or render it impure. To suggest this would be to indulge in fantastic Platonism. It would be only one step from believing, as Plato did, that the real point of music is not the sounds but the abstract relation between the lengths of the lyre strings. If there are jobs waiting for people with a command of colloquial and business French, German or Spanish, then it is the duty of schools (and polytechnics and universities) to teach this by any available means. And if they persist in teaching modern foreign languages as if the *only* point in learning them were to be able to understand the classical literature written in that language or to grasp the fundamental structures of the grammar, then they are failing to educate their pupils properly. For the life of the pupils will not be better, in regard to the competence they need, as a result of the education they have had. But of course it is true that not everyone wants to work in industry or become a bilingual secretary or a doctor or an engineer. Some people may want to work as actors or booksellers or teachers, or to pursue research into history or nuclear physics. Some people may early develop so passionate a love for pure mathematics or Greek literature that they must do these things and take the risks involved. Their work, they see, must be in these fields, whatever the financial disadvantages. So it is not that 'pure' subjects should *not* be taught at schools and universities, it is only that they should not be the only things taught. And of course, this leads to difficulties of a practical kind. For not every university, and certainly not every school, can possibly undertake everything. It seems to me that at least in towns, the possibility of changing schools in order to pursue the curriculum of his choice should be open to any pupil over the age of fifteen, perhaps earlier. But to say this is to suppose that there could be some schools which specialized in, say, music or classics or advanced mathematics, and others which did not. In practice, at present this is so, but perhaps only because some schools are still living in a grammar school tradition. The sixth form college, with all its great disadvantages (in the demoting of the truncated residual schools) may perhaps be the only solution which would give sufficient flexibility, short of a return to some modified conception of the grammar school, or a more flexible use of Colleges of Further Education, or even the deployment of the sixth forms of private schools.

Thus, in advising pupils about what careers to prepare for, schools must, if they are not to fail in their duty, consider the state of the market. But this does not entail a rigid quota-system for each of the professions. It is perfectly possible to take both the employment position and the demands of the professions into account while not totally abrogating all responsibility with regard to what is to be taught, to whom and for how long. Such rational exercises in accommodating one set of pressures and demands to others are an absolutely normal part of the task in such fields as broadcasting, retailing, and all forms of government. Why not in education too? Such compromise in the construction of a curriculum may be unexciting; but it is realistic, and the resulting curriculum would satisfy the criterion we are considering: it would open the possibility for those following it of a better life than they would have had without it.

One further consequence follows from the suggestion that work is an essential part of the good life. Children do not always, or very often, like hard work. But it is not to be supposed that their tastes in childhood necessarily reflect their taste and desires in later life. There is something to be said for guiding their childhood choices as to what they will want to do later, and also for getting them as far as possible into the way of working, and admitting that it can be pleasurable, while they are still at school. This sounds so obvious that it should not even need to be said. And it would be generally agreed. But not everything that children do with energy and enthusiasm counts as work. For work, there needs to be a certain element of effort towards a goal, which *can* be reached, but may be missed. There needs to be a distinction between success and failure, between a satisfactory and a less than satisfactory outcome. And some children at school are deprived in various ways of the satisfaction of hard work. It should not be forgotten that mastery, reducing things to order, learning to be able to do things well, simply getting things right, are real pleasures. Indeed if Nietzsche was right, these things constitute almost the whole of human motivation. It is better that children should exercise the will to power in these ultimately more desirable directions than in the direction of shorter-term, more violent and destructive goals.

What, then, is to be included in this future-directed curriculum? For a start, of course, reading and writing and mathematics, especially arithmetic, to a standard of competence. Then, at the same time, such studies as will lead the pupil to some understanding, according to his capacity, of what society it is that he will be entering as a grown-up and a worker. This, above all, means some notion of the development historically of the institutions among which, and subject to which, he lives. How far he will go in this, to what extent he will branch out into economics, geography, classical history or sociology will depend on his interests and his ability. Then, if he is able to, he should have a speaking knowledge of at least one language other than his own. And he must have a certain understanding, part practical, part theoretical, of the physical sciences and technology. To live among cars, television sets and all kinds of electronic apparatus without any notion of the theory or practice of their construction is to be in an important way uneducated, and undoubtedly limits the possibilities open to him in the world of work. So, suddenly, the school timetable is pretty full. The crucial demand is that these subjects, however divided up or linked together should be taught so thoroughly that those who want to go on with them, or branch out from them into neighbouring fields will have the competence to do so. Some pupils will not go so far or so fast as others. But they must not be allowed to hold up their colleagues. Their curriculum will be the same. It will simply be that they do not proceed so far along it. But the curriculum itself should not be tempered to the shorn lamb, however sympathetic we may feel towards him. Everyone, even the quick and the able, must experience the benefits of *present* hard work, while they are still at school.

But such a programme, though it is a start, has by no means completely satisfied the criterion of preparing pupils for a good life. A whole dimension of education has been omitted, perhaps the most important of all. The scheme so far is ruthlessly utilitarian. We must consider, finally, the other great goal of education.

(c) IMAGINATION

Work, I have argued, is one of the things we value both for itself and for its consequences; it is not merely a means to an end but a goal within which means and ends cannot, in all cases, be completely distinguished. The other goal of education is again one within which the distinction between means and ends has no place, and that is the cultivation of the imagination.

In discussing this aspect of education, I shall make certain assumptions about imagination, for which I have argued elsewhere. I use the term to cover a human capacity shared by everyone who can perceive and think, who can notice things and can experience emotions (that is by virtually everyone who is subject to education, only the most grossly mentally handicapped being, possibly, excluded). Imagination in this sense is involved in all perception of the world, in that it is that element in perception which makes what we see and hear meaningful to us. It is the element, that is, by means of which we characterize and feel things to be familiar, unfamiliar, beautiful, desirable, strange, horrible, and so on. Being the image-making capacity, it is also involved in memory of the past and the envisaging of the future, as well as in that kind of dreaming and day-dreaming which is neither memory nor prediction, but fantasy. Its connexion, therefore, with creativity, and especially with artistic creation, is central; but its exercise is by no means confined to this. Those who perceive, dream or remember with heightened imagination may, often do, long to express in some form what it is that they perceive, but they may not necessarily even try to do so. However, the creative character of imagination is manifest, even if nothing is 'made' except the significance or meaning to the observer of the world he perceives. In that everybody inhabits a world which has some meaning, everyone possesses imagination. And this is proved, even if the meanings are perfectly ordinary, for instance, that this is an object which could be used as a tool; that this is a table which has always stood in the same place. But deeper reflection, noticing more, thinking about things more consistently, feeling about them more strongly, these are all things we can learn to do, and all of them increase the significance of the world we live in. The concept of imagination, as I here employ it, is not particularly eccentric. I think it will be clear that it is related to the concept as analysed by philosophers such as Hume and Kant and Wittgenstein. It is also close to the sense in which Shelley spoke of the imagination as that which made love and sympathy possible, and in which Coleridge, describing Wordsworth in *Biographia Literaria* spoke of the 'union of deep feeling with profound thought, the fine balance of truth in observing with the . . . faculty of modifying the objects observed'. Educating a child's imagination, then, is partly educating his reflective capacity, partly his perceptive capacity; it may or may not lead to 'creativity'; but it will certainly lead to his inhabiting a world more interesting, better loved and understood, less boring, than if he had not been so educated.

Being more imaginative, is, I believe, like being more healthy. There is no need to raise the question 'Why do you want it?' or 'How does it benefit you?' If you know what 'being healthy' means, you know that it is desirable, and desirable both for its own sake and for its consequences. This was a platitude for the Greeks and is so for us. Analogously, while everyone exercises imagination in some degree, the desirability of exercising it more is not to be defended on the grounds that it leads to anything good, though it may well do so, but simply on the grounds that, if understood, it will be seen to *be* good. Thus it becomes clear that if a particular study can be shown to increase the imaginative powers of a child, then it is a strong candidate for inclusion in the educational curriculum, granted that the point of that curriculum is to offer to the child the possibility of a better life than he could have had without it. So it is necessary next to consider what kinds of studies can be described as imagination-enhancing.

The test here may at first sight seem frivolous, but I believe that, if properly considered, it is the very opposite: the test is whether or not the educational curriculum is boring. If we consider young children, it is a familiar fact that play is educational and is the crucially important way in which they learn to understand the world, and that play is connected with the learning of language, both because both go on at the same time, and because exploring the uses of language is itself a kind of free play. But play and language-learning both need stimulus, and in the absence of it boredom descends quite suddenly on children, like the onset of a disease, and the pleasure of play is instantly blotted out. So school can at first be seen as a kind of institutionalized stimulus, to prevent the sudden and sporadic removal of the motive to go on, such as is familiar among children left to themselves.

Gradually, school can become more and more explicit about

the learning, and the emphasis on *what* is to be learned can be increased, so that somewhere along the line the distinction between work and play becomes familiar, as does the distinction between really doing things and pretending to do them. This, educationally, is a crucial distinction, and it involves attitudes and emotions which may have long-term effects on people's lives (though they need not be unchangeable or fixed). Of course it is a platitude to say that one should concentrate, eventually, on work with the same sort of enthusiasm as was originally given to play. But the difference is that, in the case of work, there is an additional motive to go on with it even when, with all available stimulation, the pleasure may have palled.

Ideally, both work and play should be equally absorbing. The obstacle to finding either so is that it should seem futile or pointless. Now one danger at school is that the distinction between work and play may be introduced too late, or too confusedly, perhaps through fear of turning pupils against what is described as work, or allowing them to feel they may give up what is described as play when they are tired of it. For play is attractive only so long as the agent *wants* to play. It is fun as long as it is enjoyed (and not a moment longer) and its only justification is that it is fun. So being told that something is fun (and therefore being made to believe it is play) can be damagingly misleading, if when one wants to stop doing it, because it is not fun, one is told one has to go on. Far better to be told that the activity in question is work, may or may not be fun, but that in any case one has to do it, on other grounds.

For what one does at school must at all costs be *felt* to have some point; and that point may be either intrinsic (it is fun to do) or extrinsic (it is worth doing as a means to something else) or, of course, both. A great deal of what is learned at school ought to be justified, as we have seen, on the grounds that unless it is learned, other things cannot be done or understood. This is, after all, the attitude quite naturally adopted by grown-ups who, wanting later in life to attain some educational qualification, go through various preliminaries in order to get what they want. There is no reason why even quite young children cannot adopt the same attitude, and many of them do. But enough has been said of these instrumental components of the curriculum already.

The crucial extra fact is that doing something because it is useful does not rule out the possibility of enjoying it. Rather the reverse. For if one does it on the grounds that it is useful, one does it *properly*. And it is only in the course of doing things like reading, learning a musical instrument, or cooking properly that one begins to understand what the pleasure of them is. It is this which explains the curious pedagogical fact that it is often in teaching a class who are studying a subject for no other reason than that they need to pass an examination in it for some particular purpose that one actually encounters most pleasure in the subject (that is, unless the examination is a very bad and foolish one). For the fact that the pupils have simply got to get down to it and learn about the subject in some detail ensures that they will begin to see how interesting the subject is. This is the connexion, then, between work and the imagination. For the imagination is the power to see possibilities, beyond the immediate; to perceive and feel the boundlessness of what is before one, the intricacies of a problem, the complications or subtleties of something previously scarcely noticed. To work at something, to begin to find it interesting, this is to begin to let the imagination play on it. To begin to explore something imaginatively is to begin to see it stretching out into *un*explored paths, whose ends are not in sight. So what school must offer is the chance to concentrate, whether on play or, equally, on work recognized as work, even if from time to time it seems uncongenial, merely a necessary task to be got through.

But in order to ensure that there is something that a child will learn to love, to want to do properly for its own sake while he he is still at school, it is necessary that within the framework of a work-orientated curriculum, he should be able to choose some of the things he does, and in some areas at least to follow his bent. This means that there must be a wide variety of optional subjects at school from which he can choose as soon as he knows clearly what he likes and dislikes, and that these must be not merely 'free-time' activities, but real, hard, possibly examinable subjects, though by no means necessarily academic. We have seen already (page 149) that there are practical difficulties about ensuring that such a choice is open. But we must say something, as well, about the theoretical objections often raised against such choices. For it is said that no one while still at a school ought to have to make such radical choices as, for instance, to abandon biology and take up the trombone, or give up any but basic mathematics in favour of Greek. It is argued (for example by Hirst) that all pupils ought to know something about everything; and it is often taken for granted that specialization is intrinsically evil.

If the argument against specialization is that it is very difficult for children, even with good advice, to make up their minds, then this must be allowed. But choices are often difficult, especially if much is on offer, and this would not by itself be a good argument against specialization. If the argument is rather that they may regret later the choice they made so young, then this would be partly answered as I suggested (page 148) by a system within which one could go back into education from time to time, and do things one had decided against doing earlier. To work out such a system, which is urgently needed and highly desirable (and ought not to be bleakly referred to as 'retraining') is a matter of educational administration rather than curriculum planning. But if it is genuinely argued that 'broadness' is an overriding educational aim, then I have never yet seen a convincing argument to show that it is better to leave school with a smattering of superficial knowledge of economics, sociology, physics, French literature, geography and so on than with one genuine enthusiasm.

There are many arguments against the smattering programme, popular though its defence is, not least the argument that within such a programme the pupil is totally at the mercy of the teacher. He can never get to know enough of the seven forms of knowledge (or however many there are) to be able to criticize his teacher's views; he is bound to accept the terminology, the 'framework' and the carefully chosen examples, lock, stock and barrel. There just is not time for more. So the risks of dogmatism on the part of the teachers, the handing on of traditional or trendy views uncriticized, is greater with every increase of 'width' or 'breadth' in the curriculum.

But my main argument is the argument from boredom. Given that the imagination is that which enables our mind to rest upon a particular object or phenomenon and see where it leads and what its point is, then the programme of acquiring a bowing acquaintance with a number of different subjects without stopping on any of them, or of treating all branches of knowledge as one vast undifferentiated subject area, must, either of them, be anti-imaginative. And granted that the imagination is by definition not bounded by what is immediately before it, then anyone who is exercising his imagination on what he is doing is necessarily not bored at the moment that he is doing it. So there is a strong likelihood that specialization will be less boring, will give greater play to the imagination, than its opposite. For it certainly is not the case that being told by someone else what a subject is like is the true way to produce either understanding or enthusiasm. It is only by considering a thing deeply and for its own sake that one can properly begin to enjoy or understand it.

Moreover, and incidentally, it is far more likely that pupils at school will learn the essential skills of communication, and, equally important, of taking part in a genuine exchange of ideas and information, if they are becoming specialists and enthusiasts about some subject matter, whatever it is. A great deal of the inability to write coherently comes I suspect, through never having been obliged to write something short, clear and explanatory about a subject of which one is a master, or is near to becoming one. Nothing is so likely to produce an apparently inarticulate, mindless adolescent as being constantly obliged to contribute to discussion of subject matter with regard to which he is totally ignorant or absolutely uninterested.

Of course I am not arguing that it is undesirable to know about a great many different things. On the contrary, it is certainly desirable. It is simply that if the range of subjects a pupil has to learn at school is too great, then his imagination cannot be fired by any of them in such a way that he realizes what possibilities there are for him to explore. The prepackaged, topic-centred course; the endless second-order lessons about the nature of scientific thinking as such, even if neatly illustrated by one example from physics and one from biology; the illustrations of the differences between one language and another; none of these can take the place of something definite, concrete, detailed and exact, something to master and get right. To use the imagination is to exercise it upon objects which are worthy of its attention; but absolutely anything may turn out to be worthy of attention if pursued in detail, rather than superficially. It is paradoxical that we are all ready to praise and admire a child who gets a craze for something and pursues it outside the classroom. But we make it almost impossible for him to pursue his crazes, or even acquire them, in the classroom itself, where he would ideally have so many more resources and so much more time to do what he was interested in.

There can be no doubt that the cultivation of the imagination demands that there should be time and scope for pupils to pursue their own bent while still at school, and this means to specialize. But, it may be argued, this has very little to do with the imagination as most people conceive it. Is allowing a child to become a relative specialist in mathematics or physics really to cultivate his imagination? Should not the argument rather be concerned with educating children in the creative arts? Up to a point I would agree. Obviously one whole range of subjects which satisfies our criterion (of preparing for and being part of the good life) is the vast range of the arts. And no school curriculum could possibly be complete or satisfactory which did not take education in the arts as seriously as education in other subjects, such as physics and languages. This means that all children at school should receive some education in the arts, and those who want to should become experts in these. But there is room for perhaps a little more exactitude about what such education should be.

It is often assumed that the main purpose of school arts programmes must be to develop a child's creative powers. This, it seems to me, is a mistake. The view I refer to is eloquently argued by Malcolm Ross who wrote a Schools Council Working Paper (No. 54, November 1975) entitled *Arts and the Adolescent*. In this paper he rightly deplores the low status of the arts in some secondary schools, and raises the interesting question whether better education in the arts might not sometimes do more good than pastoral or counselling services, which seem to have been relatively ineffective in improving the attitudes and the motivation of adolescents at school. He says 'The arts curriculum must have its roots in the immediate sensory experience of the individual. Its starting point must be the resensitizing and retraining of the senses themselves: the basic source of perception.' And he rightly connects sensitive perception with feeling. 'It is precisely because they have always offered men the means of realizing their feelings, of finding their way in and so possessing this world that is unique to each of us that the arts are of such critical importance in the field of education.' Here he seems to me, though using other words, exactly to be identifying the education of the imagination. But he goes on to draw the conclusion that 'the prime concern of the arts curriculum should be with the emotional development of the child *through creative self-expression*' (my italics). Why only through creative self-expression? Why not through an increased awareness of human feelings and potentialities, including his own, that comes with knowledge of what other people have written, painted, built or composed? To perceive and feel the power of great works of art, even of less than great works, is indeed to become acquainted with one's own feelings and those of mankind as a whole; it is to begin to grasp the infinite complexity and the astonishing possibilities of human nature and nature at large. It is the way, above all, in which the imagination expands, and feels both that it is a common shared power and that it is free. In all these ways to love art is to love humanity, and therefore may well be beneficial, better than counselling. To feel any such pleasure is good.

Now it is very likely that those children at school who are

excited by any form of art will want to express this excitement, and try their hand at doing what they begin to understand can be done. And it is certain that such children should be encouraged in every possible way. But it may be disastrous for education in the arts if self-expression is taken to be the sole criterion of a good arts education curriculum. To be *forced* to express oneself in an artistic medium is absurd, especially if one is supposed, in doing so, to be producing something 'expressive', 'spontaneous' or 'original'. (Trying to do or make things which are *not* 'self-expressive' is a different matter.) While teachers are flogging their pupils into original compositions, may not masterpieces of music or painting or literature go unobserved, works without the knowledge of which it is impossible to imagine a real (rather than a pretend) painter or writer getting to work; works, moreover, pleasure in which may last, or open up the way to further and greater enjoyment throughout a child's life. Let us by all means hope that pupils at school will produce expressive and original works; but let us not suppose that to induce them to do so is the whole function of aesthetic education. To see, to look, to listen, to understand, these are things which all children need to be taught to do and which we cannot neglect, if we are to teach them to enjoy their potential imaginative power.

I believe that lurking behind the 'expressive' theory of education in the arts there are two arguments. The first is a kind of therapeutic view of self-expression (and this is the view of Malcolm Ross). It will solve a child's problems if he can express himself. Therapeutic drama, writing, pottery, painting, even music is introduced into the curriculum in order to allow the child to solve practical problems in the treatment of his medium, and also to 'act out' his aggression or confusion or hatred or love. It is difficult to tell in general how effective such therapy is. But effective or not, it seems to me absolutely clear that not all children are in need of therapy; and that, even if they were, education and therapy should be distinguished (with the proviso that sometimes education may be a good form of therapy). The second argument is, roughly, egalitarian. It is thought that to educate children to appreciate and love the works of others is necessarily to teach them a 'middle-class' culture; that getting them to listen to and perform music is necessarily to get them to listen to late Beethoven quartets, and to play the 'cello, and these are thought to be bourgeois or élitist tastes. But, whether or not Beethoven and the 'cello are bourgeois, it is not necessary to confine musical education to such elements, any more than reading must be only of Shakespeare. Nor is it by any means necessary that a teacher should impose his tastes on his pupils, though he may hope to communicate them. He may learn from their tastes as well.

However, in the case of all the arts there is no doubt that the teacher will be in a position to direct the attention of his pupils to things which they would not otherwise see, hear or read. And this will entail more than just saying 'here is this book, read it'. It will, at least sometimes, involve explanation, pointing out things a child might not notice, and giving him some historical perspective on the object of his attention. After all, if imagination is the seeing or hearing *in* what is presented to us of more than would immediately meet the eye or ear, then the educated eye and ear will do better, will find more in the objects and make more sense of them than will the uneducated. To hear a melody as a melody at all, not mere sounds, to hear it as in a particular key, to hear it as a variation on a theme, to hear it as expressive, to do all these things depends on the power of imaginative interpretation, and all are better done with the help of education.

Moreover, the teacher will hope by practice to induce in the child a habit of reading, looking and listening. The ideal of such teaching is no doubt to share a pleasure. But even where the pleasure is not shared the understanding may be. And this understanding arises out of *thoughtful* perception. It is a matter of attending, and thus of practice. Neither desire for equality nor for bringing about some sort of cure should be allowed to distort the picture of what education in the arts should include. Nor should either of these desires be allowed to blind one to the real advantages in the education of the imagination to be found in contemplating the triumphs of creativity, the monuments to the imagination of other people.

It is worth adding that the contemplation of natural beauty is as central to the education of the imagination as the contemplation of works of art, and is something for which all children should somehow be given the opportunity, if only occasionally The practice of taking urban children out of school for a week at a time to stay in hostels in the country, recommended and practised by some Local Authorities as a means of social education, is equally to be recommended from this point of view. The whole school will not be Wordsworths. But that is not necessary. The direct experience of natural beauty can be as crucial to the imaginative development of any child as it was to Wordsworth, and the forming of images, their retention by the 'inner eye', their interpretation, their *feeling*, can be as valuable to anyone as it was to him. It is genuine deprivation if a child has no opportunity ever to listen to 'sounds that are the ghostly language of the ancient earth' nor to retain 'the obscure sense of possible sublimity' which the experience of natural phenomena can give. It is sad that such acts of attention and contemplation, whether of nature or of art, should have come to be thought of as 'middle class', or as academic, and suitable only for an élite of intellectuals. For such learning is in fact no more essentially intellectual than is the learning about other people which comes from friendship, is indeed very closely analogous to it. It has nothing necessarily to do with criticism or scholarship, though it may lead on to these in some cases. But the *first* point of reading, listening and looking is to learn to feel, and to feel in a way that will be a perennial source of pleasure.

Finally, if, as I have argued, it is on the education of the imagination that we must concentrate as one vast factor in constructing the school curriculum; if it is this that will above all ensure the absence of boredom and ennui for the rest of a child's life, not just his life at school, then there is one commodity which must somehow be provided at school, and that is a modicum of solitude. It seems self-evident that the imagination works surreptitiously and quietly, in the contemplation of its objects and in the reflecting on them over and over again. The 'inner eye' is a metaphor which it is hard to avoid in discussing imagination; and to use this eye, to allow its somewhat mysterious function, one must have peace and quiet. In society at large the cultivation of solitude is rare. The whole amazing growth of 'teenage culture' is against it. It is largely assumed by adolescents, and certainly by those who write for them, that spending time alone is a disaster, to be tolerated only in exceptional circumstances, or if there is some vital solitary task (like putting on a face-pack) which needs to be done. Long solitary walks may be included in some kinds of romantic mythology, but they are hardly ever undertaken, either in urban or rural life. If it is necessary, therefore, for the growth of imagination, that children should be able to be alone, and enjoy solitude, this possibility must somehow be preserved at school, even though actual physical solitude is most unlikely to be achieved there. What is perhaps a good substitute is the provision of occasions when it is perfectly appropriate for a child's mind to wander, for him to think and feel as he likes. This point has been treated already in Chapter II (page 69). Here I would just like to repeat that routine, ritual and expected forms of behaviour may contribute greatly to the peacefulness necessary for the imagination to grow, to form its images and to feel their significance. It may seem paradoxical to suggest that a certain kind of boredom can operate as an antidote to boredom, but there is truth in it all the same. It is not only that in a lesson in which one is being taught in an orderly and disciplined way, one may actually have time to think about something quite different, to allow one's mind to be partially on what is going on, partially on something else, no bad way to learn, very often. But, more, the familiarity and the safety of accustomed rituals can allow great freedom to the thoughts and feelings, and act as a source of refreshment. It would be the greatest pity, therefore, if a school curriculum were to be constructed which contained no element of the routine and the anticipated, if all teaching were abandoned in the old sense, if all work were co-operative, and even school assembly were voluntary, and geared entirely to the possibilities of participation among those who chose to attend.

I have argued that children at school should have some freedom of choice with regard to what they study; they should, as far as they can, be encouraged to follow their bent, to become experts, even if this is in a relatively narrow field; they should have and follow enthusiasms and learn to read intelligently and write clearly about things which in fact interest them. But on the other hand, if everything is a matter of choice, the security without which they cannot think and feel except superficially cannot be achieved. Even within their chosen fields, I suggest, much of their teaching should be 'formal' and the element of compulsion should not be deliberately removed. For the whole purpose of educating the imagination is that it should be able to play upon what is *given*, to concentrate on what is before it and interpret it, not in any particular way, but freely. Children need help in order to concentrate, and whatever the particular contents of the curriculum may be, we ought to be absolutely assured that such help is forthcoming.

We have reached the conclusion, then, that a school curriculum which is to be justified in terms of its looking towards a good life must be built up with the help of two guiding considerations. The first is that by means of it the schoolchild shall be prepared to work; the second, and not conflicting, consideration is that his imagination shall be educated in such a way that he will learn to feel the infinite complexities of the world he inhabits. Both these guides are in fact guides to freedom. The third ingredient in a good life is that it should be a morally justifiable life: the life of a virtuous person is better than that of a vicious person. And so, we argued, virtue, which can be taught, or at least learned, should be learned at school, among other places. But morality cannot be part of the curriculum in the sense of being a 'school subject' on the timetable. One can learn to be morally good in the very same way out of school as in it. (For instance, if a child spent as much time in hospital as in school, one would rightly fear for his education, but not necessarily for his *moral* education.)

It remains to see in what way the conclusions of this chapter serve to suggest answers to the questions we started with, to see whether any light has been thrown on the relation between education and politics, and whether we are in a position to reinforce the suggestion that educational philosophy is something with which everyone should be concerned.

V

Conclusion

Any discussion of educational issues will be composed largely of value judgements. So much is clear. In the most general terms, education itself is regarded as a good, a thing to be valued highly; and, more specifically, in the foregoing pages it was suggested that education was something that led to a good life, the description of which must necessarily incorporate values. Is it therefore necessarily the case that all discussions of education are political? We seem still to be in want of an acceptable way to distinguish the political from the non-political.

It is sometimes assumed, as we have seen, that all value judgements are political because it is held that politics is a matter of warring classes in society, and that value judgements are dictated by social class. So, on this view, I cannot say, 'It is wrong to steal', without uttering a political judgement. If one accepts this, then obviously all educational judgements and all educational decisions, since they have been shown to incorporate evaluations, will be political. There could be no possibility of 'keeping politics out of education' any more than politics could be kept out of aesthetics or out of morality itself. But this is a misleading use of 'politics', for it is too wide. We need to be able to distinguish political from other arguments, whereas on this view every argument is political. If on the other hand we mean by 'politics' 'party politics', then this may seem too narrow. For it may seem that no one could fail to wish politics in *this* sense to be kept out of education. If decisions as to what to teach and how to teach it were taken entirely on the basis of what would win votes or keep a particular party in power, without any more general considerations, this might perhaps be universally condemned. For, it would be said, the good of the pupils, which oughtto be the overriding consideration in coming to educational decisions, had been lost sight of, and postponed to considerations which had nothing to do with the pupils at all.

But of course, this would be too simple a criticism, though it is one which is often made. No politician, however ambitious for himself or his party, ever avows a single-minded devotion to the goal of re-election. He must claim that re-election is desirable *because* the politics of his party are good. That some policy becomes an election issue does not entail that there is no right way to judge that policy. Even those who are attempting to get elected by means of advocating it *may* believe that it can be justified on grounds independent of the whole package of party commitments. And certainly those who are not involved in advocating it, or any other policy in the course of election-eering, may decide for or against it on grounds which have nothing to do with the total package. Thus, if a particular kind of educational programme became for the time being a party political issue, there might nevertheless be ways of judging that programme which would be valid even if at another time it had ceased to be a matter of political controversy at all.

It is possible to judge that a form of education is good, absolutely. Then this very form of education may become a matter of politics, if questions have to be raised about who should have it, or how to supply it, pay for it, distribute it, and so on. The difference, in fact, between an issue which is political and one which is not, is not necessarily a permanent or intrinsic difference. It could be agreed that education was good, even that a particular form of education was better than another, and should be provided. Then subsequently a public decision might have to be taken about how much it was reasonable to spend on education, how far to support it in competition with rival goals; and at that point there would be a political issue.

It is for some such position as this that I have been arguing. For I have tried to show that considerations of equality are not sufficient to settle either how education should be administered, to whom and how much, or what should be taught. I have argued that this last question is by far the most important educational question there is, and that to settle it is to settle for some concept of a good life. Now the idea of equality, which has been shown to be insufficient, comes very near to being a purely political idea. Of course, it might be possible to argue for equality on grounds which were non-political. But it is difficult to see what such arguments would amount to. For equality and justice are, as we saw, closely connected ideas. And if, as is the case, political decisions are all of them concerned with the regulation of people's lives for a common good, with the weighing up of curtailment of liberty against the benefits of social living, with the balancing of conflicting interests in the state, then justice must be the aim most constantly referred to in the forming of political policies. And if justice, then equality. As we saw, equality is not an ideal which is ever seriously pursued to the exclusion of other ideals; nevertheless, it is an ideal which has its place in the context of the fair distribution of goods. It is, however, an ideal which is insufficient to determine what *is* good. To determine this, it is necessary to consider quite different values. These values have nothing to do with fair distribution at all. So once again it is necessary to assert that one must *first* decide what is educationally good, and *then* decide how it is right to provide this good. It is the recognition of this order of priority that leads to the plea to keep politics out of education. The plea rests on the very proper belief that we must get our thoughts about the education right *first*, and *then* argue about equality in its distribution.

But there is another sense in which politics cannot possibly be kept out. For the insistence that the most important question is the question what to teach; the belief that the determining of the school curriculum is the most crucial evaluation that has to be made, and that it has to be made on the criterion of contribution to the good life, all this suggests a paternalism which may well be abhorrent. Someone, some godlike philosopher-king, has to decide what it is good for children to be taught. So who is to do this? I have laid down that children must be taught what will enable them to work, and that they must be taught what will employ and expand their imaginative powers. But who am I to dictate to millions that these are the values which must be incorporated in the curriculum? Might not some other values seem far more important to somebody else?

Now I would not want to deny the charge of paternalism. It is obvious that if a curriculum is to be prepared and justified, then this has to be done from above. The decision to include this or that has to be taken by someone, and in the nature of the case such a decision will affect the lives of those subject to it, of people who had no part themselves in making the decision. This cannot be avoided. And if this is so, then at once there is a political question involved. Wherever paternalism is inevitable, the political question is, who is to be the father, and where does the power reside. One cannot avoid this issue by saying that politics and education are two different things and should be kept separate.

But there are two crucial points which have to be made. First, if decisions about the curriculum are value decisions, what has to be decided is what *we want* children to learn. We must try to think what it would be good that they should learn, not according to some mysterious pedagogic standard, but according to a consideration of the life they will be enabled to lead after they have left school. And this means that anyone can have views, and should have the right to make his views known, about what is the desirable kind of life. Parents, teachers, employers, politicians, university professors, all these overlapping classes of persons may have contributions to make to the vision of such a life. Moreover, they *may* know, employers and parents as much as teachers, what it is that their children need to learn if they are to live such a life. So although educational theorists and professional syllabus-constructors may have charge over the details of the syllabuses to be followed at school, on the question of the broad aims of the curriculum (the point of the child's education), there is no reason whatever to remain passively in the hands of the professionals. People who are amateurs but who are capable, as everyone is, of forming value judgements, are perfectly entitled to make their desires known, indeed to demand that education shall go the way they want, and shall prepare children for life as they want to see it lived.

So, though making curricular decisions is paternalistic with regard to the children who will follow the curriculum, it is not necessary that only one person, or one kind of person should (ultimately) wield the power. Of course, it is true that methods of making known what people want are slow and cumbersome and it is true that curricula, once made, tend to get frozen into immobility for decades. Nevertheless, society at large should not forget that at a highly general level, it is *for them*, in order to fulfil *their* wants and aspirations, that education exists. If it is a vision of the good life which ultimately determines curriculum content, then this vision cannot be imposed on people. In the long run it must be their own. It has been argued above that paternalism involves a political decision about power. It should not be forgotten that democracy is a form of politics. We may agree with Plato that what children learn is of the highest importance, but we need not agree that any philosophers can know what it is that they *should* learn.

The second point is this: I have argued for the twin values of work and the expanding imagination as the supreme determinants of curriculum content. And I have related these two values by arguing that each in a different way is to be seen as a means to freedom, or indeed as a contributing part of freedom. For the ability to work is plainly the ability to be an active agent, to change things rather than just let them happen. It is also the ability to be independent, to carve out a career or a way of life in which one is not dependent on anybody's charity. Such is the bourgeois work-ethic. To work is to control rather than be controlled. On the other hand, the imagination is the pre-condition without which any freedom is impossible. It is the means by which a future can be envisaged which is different from the present. It is the necessary condition of change, to say nothing of revolution.

To suggest that the values which must be embodied in the curriculum are values which are constitutive of freedom is to suggest the constant possibility of change. For the ability to imagine is necessary before there can be any criticism of what is currently on offer. It is only if one can imaginatively see and understand the present that one can seriously envisage ways in which it might be altered or improved, or, come to that, can formulate reasons why it should be conserved. But criticism is no good unless it is practical; and work is the practical part of life after school. The paternalism, then, which lays down these particular values is a paternalism which may at any time be overthrown. Just as the good teacher is ready to be surpassed by his pupil, the good curriculum-maker should also aim that his curriculum will be criticized and improved by those who pursue it. But the point is that they must pursue it first and criticize it afterwards. For it is only by means of single-minded devotion to the task in hand, by actually getting absorbed in the subjects in hand, whatever they are, that someone at school will learn what it is to do things properly And to teach him this, as I tried to show in Chapter IV, ought to be the common aim of all parts of the curriculum.

The curriculum at school, then, must embody the values of society; and this means that in one sense the most important educational decisions are political, in another sense they are not. It cannot be denied that these conclusions look pretty thin, and after all so obvious as to provoke derision. And perhaps they would not need to be stated at all if they were not so often denied, implicitly or explicitly. If my arguments have any validity, the most important question which has to be asked, as I have said before, is what children ought to learn at school. This is far more important than any question relating to the kinds of school they should go to, whether they should or should not be selected for different kinds of education according to ability, or whether they should continue to be educated after the age of sixteen, as of right. It is also more important than questions about teaching methods, or whether to think, organize the timetable, in terms of *subjects* or not. All these other questions become important only if the answers to them can be shown, as they very often can, to have implications with respect to the actual content of the curriculum. If it can be shown that, for example, by treating history and geography as one subject rather than as two, children can be more readily interested and can acquire more, and more useful, knowledge, then this would be an excellent reason, and the only good reason, for amalgamating the two. If it can be shown that by means of mixed-ability teaching everyone learned more, and that what they learned was more useful to them and more stimulating to their imagination, then this again would be the only good argument for introducing it universally. If having different curricula for different kinds of school deprives some children of the chance to learn the things we want them to learn, then such diversity must be abandoned.

A teacher must, according to my arguments, always raise the question whether what the children are actually learning is what they need to enable them to think and feel and work more freely. This will involve both raising the question whether the curriculum itself, as written down, is a good one (does it lay down what children in general *need* to know on any given subject? does it take things in a rational order?), and also raising the question, with regard to each child, whether he can now do more than he could, whether he knows more than he did, whether he thinks more sensitively and understands more thoroughly than he did. If all these questions are answered in the affirmative, then the curriculum is right for the child.

Moreover, if, as I have argued, the teacher is responsible not only for the child's learning what is contained in the curriculum but also, in part, for his learning to behave well, to become morally good, then the questions which he as a teacher must ask are not confined to the curriculum. He must raise the question whether this other, extra-curricular learning, is also going on. And this is a burden. If only it were true that morality could be taught by means of two periods a week with the teacher's notes, and that learning by example, or by tea and sympathy, could properly be derided or written off, then both teacher and pupil could forget morality until the next morals lesson, and things would be easier. But since it is not so, the teacher is required to have a constant awareness of how his behaviour will seem to the child. He must ask whether his own ways of settling disputes, allotting praise or blame, insisting that tasks should be completed, will seem good or bad, fair or unfair to his pupils. It is a great deal to ask. And I would in fact ask one more thing still. I would ask that the teacher should be, and should remain, interested in educational philosophy, should think about it regularly and should see whether or not what the philosophers and theorists say makes sense. For though, like all philosophy, the philosophy of education is theoretical, it has more practical bearings than most, and it arises out of, and is supposed to cast light back on to, the life of school. To this extent it can be checked against the facts. It is often urged that the philosophy of education is useful and valuable because it helps both teachers and philosophers themselves to be clear-headed about such concepts as those of 'teaching', 'learning', 'persons' and so on. Just so the philosophy of football might be thought to be an aid both to players and to sports commentators alike by clarifying the ideas of 'scoring', 'passing', 'attacking', 'defending' and so on.

But my argument would be rather different. If clarity is what is needed, then it is clarity, not so much about the abstract concepts, as about the actual point and purpose of educating children. This means that one has to think about what one hopes for them when their education is over. It is less important to form judgements about education itself than about the life to which it is all leading. Teachers should, I maintain, as much as parents and employers, be ready to say what they want. They should be ready to state what they value as a necessary part of a good life. But teachers in addition should be able to justify everything they do at school with reference to these wants and values. Only if they can do this can they be said to be attempting democratically to determine the direction of the educational curriculum. But *if* they can do it, then they will be demonstrating in a practical way what I have hoped to demonstrate on paper, that there is no way finally to separate moral, political and educational problems. There is nothing wrong with mixing politics with education. In this sense of 'politics' it is our duty only to ensure that everyone realizes the nature of the mix.

Index